The Art of Feminine Negotiation

Praise for
The Art of Feminine Negotiation

A must read! Cindy Watson provides a step-by-step guide for women on how to successfully negotiate using a simple to follow formula. She touches on important topics including mindset, dealing with self-sabotage, and fear. The excellent advice dispensed in this book will provide the reader with courage, insight and easy to follow guideposts that are certain to step up anyone's negotiation skills.

J. Paul Nadeau, former hostage negotiator and international peacekeeper, best-selling author of *Take Control of Your Life*

I don't know of anyone doing what Cindy Watson is doing. Her *The Art of Feminine Negotiation* is powerful! She brings such passion, knowledge and confidence that I would hire her in a second.

Jack Canfield, creator of *Chicken Soup for the Soul*

This book is an experience! Cindy skillfully debunks the myth that you need an aggressive, winner-take-all attitude to be an effective negotiator. With Cindy's guidance, you'll move from problems and unconscious biases women often encounter when negotiating (or choosing not to negotiate) to secret weapons and how to ask the right questions. Cindy lays out powerful frameworks in digestible chunks that are easy to understand and implement in your real life. This is a book you will share and discuss with friends!

Dr. Michele Williams, negotiation professor

This book is a "certified fresh" approach to negotiation from your living room to the boardroom. Cindy shows her insight by dropping gems the reader will truly appreciate. Trust me, AOFN is an investment you and your bookshelf will appreciate.

Isaac Betancourt, FBI-trained former hostage negotiator

The Art of Feminine Negotiation is a must-have for every woman looking to step into her power and negotiate more effectively. Cindy's framework is a unique combination of practical 'how-to' steps and an illuminating exploration of the conditioning that holds us back from asking for and getting what we want both personally and professionally. Women will come away empowered to lean in to their feminine to negotiate their best life.

Sage Lavine, CEO and best-selling author of *Women Rocking Business*

This book is a must-have for every woman looking to get more of what she deserves in life! Cindy makes the art of negotiation accessible through her simple but powerful models. More importantly, her unique approach uncovers how to be more persuasive and effective from a place of authentic feminine power. Readers will walk away feeling more confident and able to negotiate best outcomes in every area of their life. This is a game-changer!

Alina Vincent, CEO of Business Success Strategies,
Best-selling author of *Personal Paparazzi*:
Your Brand Story Told Your Way

THE ART

OF
Feminine
NEGOTIATION

HOW TO GET

WHAT YOU WANT

FROM THE BOARDROOM

TO THE BEDROOM

CINDY
WATSON

NEW YORK

LONDON • NASHVILLE • MELBOURNE • VANCOUVER

The Art of Feminine Negotiation

How to Get What You Want from the Boardroom to the Bedroom

Published in New York, New York, by Morgan James Publishing. Morgan James is a trademark of Morgan James, LLC. www.MorganJamesPublishing.com

Proudly distributed by Ingram Publisher Services.

Morgan James BOGO™

A **FREE** ebook edition is available for you or a friend with the purchase of this print book.

CLEARLY SIGN YOUR NAME ABOVE

Instructions to claim your free ebook edition:
1. Visit MorganJamesBOGO.com
2. Sign your name CLEARLY in the space above
3. Complete the form and submit a photo of this entire page
4. You or your friend can download the ebook to your preferred device

ISBN 9781631959769 paperback
ISBN 9781631959776 ebook
Library of Congress Control Number: 2022938640

Cover Design by:
Rachel Lopez
www.r2cdesign.com

Interior Design by:
Christopher Kirk
www.GFSstudio.com

Morgan James is a proud partner of Habitat for Humanity Peninsula and Greater Williamsburg. Partners in building since 2006.

Get involved today! Visit: www.morgan-james-publishing.com/giving-back

*To women everywhere ready to get what they want
from the boardroom to the bedroom.*

*And to
my husband, Don
and my children,
Jade, Chase, and Dakota,
who provided the epiphanies that made this book possible.*

Enhance Your Experience of This Book

This book is an interactive journey.
There are exercises throughout which I invite you to explore.
To further enhance your experience of this book and maximize the benefits,
so this becomes a truly life-changing event,
I also want to offer you supplementary tools.

Take advantage of the additional FREE RESOURCES
to assist you in implementing the insights you'll discover in these pages,
and to ensure you continue to reap the rewards going forward.

In additon to the bonus materials,
there's even an *Art of Feminine Negotiation Workbook*
where you can do all the exercises and answer questions from the book.

I've even included a special bonus …
FREE access to my online CONFIDENCE BOOST program!

Grab your extra RESOURCE MATERIALS at:
www.ArtOfFeminineNegotiationBook.com
so you can get more of what you want and deserve,
from the boardroom to the bedroom.

TABLE OF CONTENTS

FOREWORD

first met Cindy virtually during the height of the Covid-19 pandemic in 2020. Even though our first meeting was virtual, I was immediately struck by Cindy's passion for negotiation and by how comfortable she was in a wide variety of professional situations. I watched Cindy's confidence and compassion on panels of almost exclusively men, panels that were all women and all-women panels where she was one of the few white women. Her understanding of human nature, curiosity, and desire to help people negotiate successfully permeated those virtual stages and are assembled for you here in The Art of Feminine Negotiation.

I met Cindy after having taught negotiation for over 15 years and we connected around our passion for negotiation immediately. I started my career teaching "Power and Negotiations" in the MBA program at the MIT Sloan School of Management and years later developed a course on "Women in Leadership, Negotiation, and Entrepreneurship" at Cornell's School of Industrial and Labor Relations. Thus, Cindy, as a labor and social justice attorney, and I connected both around our passion for negotiation and our passion for making accurate information on negotiation available to all women and all people. This book does just that.

Cindy skillfully debunks the myth that you need an aggressive, winner-take-all attitude to be an effective negotiator. But is feminine power in negotiation really possible? As you read this book, Cindy will dispel any lingering doubts. You will cover problems women encounter, how unconscious bias can show up in your own mind as self-limiting beliefs as well as strategies that you can use to shift your mindset.

But don't plan to just passively read; this book is an experience! As you read, you will feel as if you're in small workshop. You will encounter real-life negotiation examples, Cindy's personal negotiations for the life of her daughter, and more.

You'll actively participate in powerful exercises that help you overcome ways of thinking that you probably didn't know were holding you back from becoming a more skillful negotiator. And every step of the way Cindy will be there to guide you.

With Cindy's guidance, you will move from problems and unconscious biases women often encounter when negotiating (or choosing not to negotiate) to secret weapons and how to ask the right questions. Cindy lays out powerful frameworks in digestible chunks that are easy to understand and implement in your real life. She helps you tackle internal negotiation pitfalls ("deadly sins" and "your internal saboteur") and then she walks you through negotiation fundamentals from prenegotiation preparation to post-negotiation follow-up.

This is a book you will share and discuss with friends! I am glad that you've selected this book and excited that you are embarking on a journey to negotiate your best life.

Michele Williams, Ph.D.
Associate Professor with Tenure
John L. Miclot Faculty Fellow in Entrepreneurship
Tippie College of Business
University of Iowa

INTRODUCTION

W hat if I suggested that women are naturally better negotiators than men? Or, at the very least, that bringing 'feminine' traits to the table enhances bargaining effectiveness. Would you balk? Reject the idea? Close the book? At a minimum, I'm sure you'd ask, "So why do women still make less money than men? Why do they typically *ask* for less than men? Why do they hesitate in speaking up?" All good questions. Important questions.

You may wonder if learning the art of negotiation (feminine or otherwise) really matters. Let's face it, we're all busy. You may be asking if this is something you should make a priority. Let me assure you it is.

All of life is a negotiation. Whether it's negotiating with your intimate partner, your kids, a boss, employees, contractors, insurance companies, banks or multi-million-dollar mergers and acquisitions. It just may be the single most important skill set you'll ever learn.

Yet we're not taught to negotiate, whether for the boardroom, the bedroom, or the spaces in between. Or, to the extent that we're taught at all, we're led to believe that negotiation is all about the bark and bite—that toughness carries the day.

Let's debunk that myth and together, tackle and uncover some of the unconscious biases that may have been holding you back from fully stepping into your feminine power. Because the truth is, when you explore the key skill sets that make and mark a great negotiator, they're skills typically considered 'feminine' traits. You undoubtedly use them in a myriad of ways every day. You probably just haven't thought of it as negotiating.

Together, in this book, we'll explore how you can tap into those strengths with intention, bring them to your day-to-day bargaining, up-level your negotiations and get what you want.

Better yet, you'll be able to get what you deserve without the winner-take-all, competitive approach that seems to prevail in many negotiations today. You'll be able to negotiate from a place of authentic feminine power to get more creative solutions, better results for all, better buy-in, longer lasting agreements, and higher satisfaction from your bargaining partners, all while building better relationships personally and professionally.

Imagine the power of that kind of bargaining in your life. Imagine the ripple effect of that kind of bargaining for the world.

A Word about Feminine Power

Before we go any further, let me clarify a possible sticking point. Did you pause when I mentioned feminine power? Wonder what I meant by that? Well, let me be clear from the outset. There is no one way to be a woman. No one way to be feminine or to bring feminine power. It means different things to different people. And that's okay. In fact, that's (in part) the point. So long as your style is true and authentic to you, and not based on unconscious biases or conditioning that may have shaped who you feel you need to show up as, that's beautiful.

When I speak of the Art of Feminine Negotiation, I'm referring to bringing those traits or energies typically considered 'feminine' (but too often ignored in bargaining) to the table with intention in your negotiations. Doing so will up-level your bargaining and increase your success.

Let me acknowledge at the outset that the use of words 'masculine' and 'feminine' is not perfect. In fact, the world is changing, and I suspect these words will soon be replaced with non-gender-associated alternatives. But they're what we have to work with now. And in a study of 64,000 people across 13 countries representing a significantly diverse range of cultural, political and economic backgrounds, there was still strong consistency in the traits the vast majority of people attributed as masculine, feminine or neutral.[1]

So, when I speak throughout the book about 'acting like a man' or when I refer to masculine or feminine qualities, this isn't intended to lump all men or women into any particular boxes, but rather, it's speaking to the currently 'perceived' masculine or feminine energy typically associated with the subject, not necessarily the gender.

And to be perfectly candid, I believe there's some value in attaching 'feminine' awareness to a subject that for too long has been viewed through a traditional masculine lens. There is arguably merit in shocking us out of our complacency as we shift to a new paradigm.

If the usage of the term 'feminine' causes some controversy, and with it increased awareness, then I'll consider that I've achieved at least one objective in putting this book out in the universe.

Rise of the Feminine

I believe this book will be a life-changing intervention for you.

The world is out of balance today. Everything is energy. And we all have both masculine and feminine energy. And yet, the feminine voice has been discounted and sometimes outright suppressed for generations.

As we came to define success based almost exclusively on a masculine model, it's no surprise that both men and women hesitate to step into their feminine strengths, believing that's the only way to succeed. They see their feminine as weakness and so eschew their feminine in favor of a more mas-culine 'take no prisoners' approach to negotiating… in business and in life. And so, we create a shift that tips the balance.

Today, we're feeling the effects of both rapid technological growth and climate change. We're seeing suicide rates at all time high levels with depression and anxiety on the rise as well—across all ages and cultures. On the global scene, people are starting to flip their perceptions, to recognize the value of the feminine voice to bring us back into balance. In fact, in the 64,000-person study mentioned above, two thirds of those surveyed across 13 countries stated they believed "the world would be a better place if men thought more like women."[2]

And in the chaos of COVID there was much talk and speculation that countries with female leaders fared best when the outbreak hit. With-out getting into the muck of whether there is statistical support for that proposition, suffice it to say that at the very least, the value of 'feminine stock' went up. Feminine traits were being recognized as strengths rather than weaknesses and the desirability of these traits in leadership—business, politics and beyond—were being touted for the first time in a long time.

I invite you to bust the myths that may have caused you to reject or stifle the full force of your feminine power.

And I believe the time is now… for you… and for the world.

What Are You Looking For?

What made you pick up this book? Is it because you feel like you're not heard? You don't feel like you have a strong enough voice? You're not get-ting the money you deserve? Or the respect? Do you shrink a little when you have to negotiate for yourself? Or at the other end of the spectrum, do you feel like you've lost yourself as you adopted a 'masculine' energy, believing that was the way to make it in a 'man's world'? Maybe it's a com-bination of these or something else altogether.

One thing I can assure you… you're not alone. Most women either feel like they don't know how to negotiate, or feel they have to overcompensate to be heard. The good news? Neither are true.

But before we jump into the content, I'd ask you to consider, what are you hoping to get out of this book? I invite you to set an intention for yourself about what you desire to achieve and take away.

Setting an intention in advance will deepen the experience and learning as it opens your receptivity and sets your rudder to help you navigate these waters in a way that's meaningful for you. After all, I don't want you feeling like you're lost at sea without a nautical chart.

What's your intention?

How Are You Going to Get It?

If your end goal is to come away a more powerful negotiator, better able to ask for and get what you want in life, both personally and professionally, then you've come to the right place. You'll get that in spades… and then some!

Before we dig in to the nuts and bolts of *how* to negotiate, we need to tackle the blocks that have likely been holding you back. We'll be taking an 'inside out' approach, starting with the psychology and working out to the pre-negotiation preparation strategies and then to the negotiation itself. The psychology is arguably more important than the mechanics.

Psychology can be your best friend or your worst enemy. All of life is a negotiation and your first and most important negotiation is with yourself. And so, I'll invite you to negotiate your mindset.

Having studied some of the most powerful performers and achievers of our generation, the ultimate advantage they have is their mindset. All success begins and ends in the mind. Let's build the right mindset to attract what we desire in our life.

ELEMENTS OF SUCCESSFUL BARGAINING

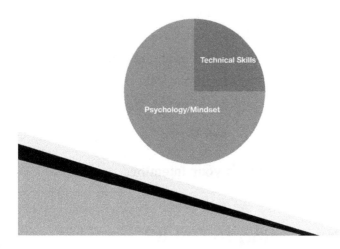

Be prepared to do both the inner and outer work. The reward will be profound mindset breakthroughs that will elevate your confidence and with it your influence and persuasive abilities.

WELCOME

Welcome to the Art of Feminine Negotiation™. I'm excited you're here—that you decided to embrace and refine your power of feminine persuasion (or HERsuasion™ as I like to call it). Congratulations for investing in yourself. Give yourself a big pat on the back. This is a big step.

Your decision to up your game is already paying dividends because it means your mindset shift has already started. That's one of many bonus side effects to believing in yourself and making a decision to step up to become the best version of you.

To reinforce that decision, I'm going to ask you to make a commitment. I want you to get the most out of this book, to own your negotiating power in a way that is most authentic for you. To do that, you'll need to play full out.

When you come across questions or challenges throughout the book, commit to them. That means not just answering the questions in your head, or worse, telling yourself you'll come back to the exercises another time. Even if the answers seem obvious or silly to you, take the time to think about them. Give the most honest responses you can.

Because I think that commitment is key, I ask you to make a Pledge to yourself.

Read it out loud.
> Sign it.
>> Feel it.

It may not seem like much, but the personal bond and declaration will help keep your feet to the fire to put in your best effort to get maximum value out of our time together.

PLEDGE
I, _____,
HEREBY PLEDGE TO PARTICIPATE FULLY
IN THIS PROCESS, TO PLAY FULL OUT,
TO THINK ABOUT THE QUESTIONS
POSED, TO DIG DEEP, TO BE RUTHLESSLY
HONEST WITH MYSELF, AND ABOVE ALL,
TO RECOGNIZE THAT I AM POWERFUL
AND I AM WORTH IT.
SIGNED THIS _____ DAY OF
_____, 20____.

_____
(Signature)

Who Am I?

You may be wondering who I am to be teaching the Art of Feminine Negotiation. Let me tell you briefly about myself, so you know a little about me, what credentials I have, and why I feel so passionately about sharing this important skill set with women.

I've been a social justice attorney for over 30 years, where I routinely negotiated high stakes, intense deals. With a specialty in union side labor law (a male dominated niche within a male dominated industry), I'm sure it won't come as a surprise that I faced a lot of gender issues. I was often the only woman in the room, whether client meetings, negotiations or hearings.

Like a lot of women, I thought I had to get tough to prove myself. And I did. I developed a reputation as a tough litigator and even tougher negotiator. But there was a high price that came with that moniker.

Before I go there, let me tell you a bit about my story. I grew up in a low rental apartment in a tough neighborhood. I never thought of it as tough at the time… it was just home.

My dad taught inner city boys to box. I'm sure he wanted boys himself, but instead, he got my sister and me. He never taught us to box, but he did teach us to fight. We had nightly spirited debates around our tiny kitchen table. I never realized until much later in life what a gift he'd given us—the belief that our voice mattered.

As with many kids who come from 'nothing', I was driven. Driven to 'succeed', to have more—more space than that little apartment, more money, but mostly, more respect. So, I went from high school to university to law school, shooting for those straight A's.

In law school, I took a negotiation course. We basically had to negotiate for our marks as we were broken into pairs to face-off against each other in a series of simulated exercises. If you didn't get a deal in the one-hour class time, you got a zero. The person with the highest monetary settlement in the class got the highest mark and so on down to the lowest. There was no room for creative outside-the-box solutions.

I didn't realize it at the time, but back then I was negotiating from what I later came to recognize as my authentic place of—dare I say—feminine power. I didn't come to those negotiations looking to put one over on my classmates, or run roughshod over them, or bully them, or leave nothing on the table. I came to each negotiation looking to build trust and rapport, being flexible, using my intuition and empathy, trying to find out what they needed and how we could get them there in a way where we both won.

I hadn't been taught to negotiate. This came naturally. It was my intuitive approach to bargaining. And I won virtually every simulated exercise that year.

But then I started the practice of law. As the only woman in the room, I quickly came to believe that to be accepted I needed to be tougher. I got approbation when I ripped the other side apart on cross-examination, when I pushed for every last penny and then some. I still got great results, but I'd lost my intuitive feminine style.

My clients called me 'The Barracuda". They meant it as a compliment, and in my naiveté, I took it as a compliment for the longest time. Heck, I wore it like a badge of honor. Until it started seeping into my other relationships, affecting my very sense of self. But it happened slowly. So slowly, that like the proverbial frog in the boiling water, I didn't notice until I'd lost pieces of myself and woke up not recognizing the woman in the mirror.

And it was then that I thought back to that negotiation course. And I remembered that I'd been a really effective negotiator when I was my authentic self, when I drew on my 'feminine' strengths. I realized I'd been duped into believing that to be effective, to get ahead, to get what I wanted, I needed to act 'like a man'. And I realized it wasn't true. I didn't have to. And neither do you. Let me show you how.

What's your story?
What's been your experience around negotiations?
What made you pick up this book?

PROBLEMS & PERCEPTION

P resumably you're here because you feel like you need to hone your negotiation skills so you can get more of what you deserve in life. You're not alone. Many women hesitate to speak up, believing they're not effective negotiators (or alternatively, as with my experience, they feel they need to negotiate aggressively to be effective, even if that's not their natural authentic style).

Most women make less money than their male counterparts. By way of context, while the gap is thinning in California, at the other end of the spectrum the wage disparity is significant in the U.S., with women making as little as 69% compared to their male counterparts.[3] When part-time workers are factored in (who are predominantly women) the gap widens.[4] For women of color, there's an even bigger gap. In the U.S., black women are paid just 61 cents for every dollar paid to white men; indigenous women are paid 58 cents on the dollar; and Latina women are paid only 53 cents for every dollar their male counterparts earn. Canada doesn't fare much better with racialized women earning only 67% of their white male counterparts and indigenous women earning only 65%. And women with disabilities earn only 54% as compared to their white male counterparts. On top of that, women typically get lower starting salaries.[5] The cherry on this nasty sundae is that they're less likely to get promotions as well.

You may be thinking that it's unfair for me to sit in judgment because surely negotiation comes easy to attorneys. What could a lawyer possibly understand about the problems for women as negotiators in life? Well, you may be surprised to hear that female attorneys don't fare any better for themselves in this arena. Evidently women in law don't self-advocate enough either.

In a 2014 American Bar Association review, female attorneys earned only 72.4% of their male counterparts' salaries. You may expect that this disparity would resolve itself as we go higher up the food chain. Sadly not. In fact, the stats get worse as we go higher up the law firm hierarchy.[6] There was a 53% pay gap between male and female partners in the top U.S law firms and incredibly it seems that gap is widening.[7]

Why is that? What holds women back? What are some of our barriers? What limits us—both internally and externally?

Let's explore the problem and its origins. Because knowledge is power. Awareness is the first step to overcoming the problem.

Are you ready to take that first step?

I. Women Don't Ask

One major hurdle facing women as negotiators is that we don't ask for what we want. Simply put, women don't ask *often* enough. And we don't ask *for* enough. Statistics show that over 57% of men ask for more money when presented with a job offer as compared to only 7% of women. Of the rarified 7% of women who do ask, they still ask for less on average.[8]

Further, not only do women avoid asking for more money, but women don't apply for jobs at all in many cases (which is another form of not asking). Research suggests that women with 80% of an identified skillset for an advertised position are less likely to apply than men with only 60% of the identified skillset.[9]

Why? For one thing, it seems that women have lower aspirational levels than men. In fact, sadly, women are 45% more likely to think that they can't change their circumstances.[10] Think about the consequences of that for a moment. How effective a negotiator are you likely to be if you go in already believing you can't change your circumstances?

These lower aspirational levels arise in part from a depleted sense of our value. We're programmed by generations of social conditioning to keep ourselves small, not rock the boat, and to feel 'less than'. We'll discuss social conditioning more fully below.

Additionally, women tend to be held back by conditioned fears. We'll discuss the impact of fear on negotiations later, but for now, it's worth noting that fear of rejection, fear of getting that 'no', and fear of being judged are major culprits contributing to our failure to ask for what we want.

Don't panic. As I said earlier, awareness is the first key step to redressing the problem. For now, we're just identifying the problems, raising our awareness. But in the coming segments I'm going to give you hands on tips and tools to overcome these problems.

The irony is that studies consistently suggest that people who ask for more, get it.[11] I've experienced this firsthand. A good friend of mine modelled this beautifully. Like me, she came from a low-income, working class family and background. In spite of that (or maybe because of it) she was fearless about asking for what she wanted. We would go to TIFF (Toronto International Film Festival) events and she was absolutely unapologetic about asking for everything from VIP passes, chic giveaway perks intended for the stars, invitations to exclusive parties with Hollywood big names and more. And 9 times out of 10 we'd get them. Most people would hesitate to ask for fear of being rejected. But think about how much richer her experiences were simply for having asked for what she wanted.

Walking through the hotel lobby at one of these events, I noticed Colin Farrell pass us. I whispered to ask my friend if she'd noticed. She hadn't. But with no hesitation, she turned and rushed to the elevator bank where he was boarding, stuck her hand in to stop the doors closing, jumped in, proceeded to do a selfie photo-shoot and engage in animated conversation with Colin as she rode the elevator to his floor. I was a huge Colin Farrell fan, yet I stood stupefied in the lobby, waiting for her return, too embarassed to have made the ask.

This hesitation to ask shows up for women in a myriad of ways, both personally and professionally… from failing to ask for training opportunities, more money, promotions, or better job titles in the workplace to items as simple as asking for help with household chores or ensuring we get the gifts we want.

Being able to ask for what you want and need in the workplace is an area where most women can level up. One of my clients, in an executive level position, was getting dumped with all the administrative duties on top of her regular duties. Her male counterparts were not. It's worth noting that women often get tasked with these non-promotable admin duties and are disadvantaged vis-a-vis their male coworkers as a result. In our work together, she was able to get recognition for these previously discounted duties and also ask for and achieve a more equitable distribution of the tasks, thereby freeing herself up to focus on projects that catapulted her career.

Another client came to me on the verge of quitting her job, having suffered sexual harassment in the workplace for some time. As the only woman in her department, she was reluctant to speak up given little support from co-workers. After working with me, she not only spoke up and successfully achieved the removal of the offending harasser from the workplace altogether, but she became the Vice President of their high profile, male-dominated Union, effecting profound positive change in that position until her retirement many years later.

I invite you to open yourself up to explore the reasons that hold you back from asking for what you want and deserve in life. Because failing to ask for what you want is a triple whammy. Not only does it cause you to *get* less, but it makes you *feel* 'less than', and it typically leads to resentment and compromised relationships. This triple threat ultimately adversely impacts almost every aspect of your life.

~~~

Make a list of times when you haven't asked
for what you want, or what you deserve.
Think outside the box here. Don't limit yourself.
Consider your relationship with your partner, your
kids, your boss, your employees, your friends & family,
coworkers, community partners... you get the idea.
Think of some things you want in your life right now.
List what they are.
Think about who and how you could ask for them.

~~~

Don't worry. There's no wrong answer here. Only you know what you want. The point is to get you used to thinking about what you want and how to start asking for it. Now is not the time to be shy. Now is the time to start pushing a little outside your comfort zone. By all means, list some of the low hanging fruit that you know is within your easy sights. But don't be afraid of big asks too. Knock yourself out putting together your ask 'wish list'.

II. Social Conditioning and Unconscious Gender Bias

Now, let's dig a little deeper to find out why women are plagued by this resistance to asking for what we want and deserve. The impact of social expectation and conditioning cannot be overstated here. Unconscious bias seems to be the new buzz phrase. As with many trendy new concepts, it runs the risk of being trivialized. I invite you to refrain from dismissing the power of unconscious gender bias. It's worth excavating to uncover and bring to light the potentially profound undermining impact it can have on our lives as women.

As noted earlier, many women tend to shy away from negotiation, believing they're not effective, or alternatively overcompensate, believing they need to bring masculine energy to succeed. In developing my HERsuasion™ and Art of Feminine Negotiation™ programs, I was determined to delve into the *why* for this phenomenon. Turned out these unconscious gender biases were one of the key things holding women back. They encourage us to make ourselves smaller, undercut our performance, affect the choices we make, and limit our opportunities.

Isn't it time we address the monster under the bed head-on and take its power away? At the very least, it's worth taking a look at.

(i) Making Ourselves Smaller

Studies show that as early as kindergarten, young girls learn to start making themselves smaller.[12] Young boys gain social status in the schoolyard when they brag about themselves and strive to make themselves bigger than life. By contrast, as young girls, we tune in quickly to subtle and not so subtle cues that we need to step back from our young feminine power or face social shunning[13].

And so, from a young age we too often start diminishing ourselves, conditioned to be self-effacing and self-deprecating. Not exactly a recipe to allow us to step into our power, strength or confidence. It keeps us small.

This pattern dogs us as we grow. When we see ourselves as being 'too much' we feel the need to tone down. When we're a little flamboyant, whether in our dress, self-expression, or voices, we get put down. And sadly, it's often from our own gender. Remember hearing (or saying) "she's so full of herself," or some similar eviscerating refrain?

We shame ourselves about our physical attributes, our dress, our life choices—even our exuberance. We change our conduct, change our very sense of self because we fear the judgment. We don't want to be seen as too nasty, too trashy, or just plain too much.

If we're really honest with ourselves, we've all been guilty of it at one or both ends. For myself, I was aware of it at some level and fought against it, but still sometimes fell victim to the shrinking syndrome. I always loved to dance. I felt great joy in dancing with total abandon. But in my clubbing days as a young woman, I'd notice the looks, hear the comments, and feel the inhibition creep in, the need to tone down. In toning down, I became a lesser version of myself.

Is it any surprise that still later, whether in our personal or professional lives, we change our tone to avoid being seen as too aggressive? We hesitate to speak up, to ask for what we really want? Or we let men take credit for our ideas?

Can you think of times in your life when you pulled in the reins, didn't feel comfortable being your full expressive self, and/or dimmed your light in some way?

And as we dim ourselves, men are rewarded for beating their chests. They get the promotions. They get the higher wages. They get the higher ground in relationships. Because, unlike us, they put themselves out there. They expect to get what they want. They ask for what they want.

By contrast, we hold ourselves back because that conditioned little girl from the schoolyard whispers in our ear that we better not think too much of our self or there's going to be social consequences. And so, we make ourselves a little less than. Or maybe we already believe we're a little less than. Either way, we end up getting less than we deserve.

(ii) Undercutting Our Own Performance

We often hear about gender bias and assume it means bias imposed *by* men *against* women. But what about women's own internal biases? It's these insidious biases against our own gender that perhaps do the most damage. Study after study has shown that when women are primed based on their gender, they perform worse. What do I mean by that?

In a study of a group of young women taking their SAT tests, where half the control group were asked to identify their gender—simply identify whether they're male or female—that half performed more poorly than those who didn't have to identify their gender. In fact, in a Harvard study of Asian-American students, the young women performed *better* when they had to identify their *ethnicity* but *worse* when they had to identify their *gender*.[14] Similarly, a national U.S study of students taking AP calculus showed that the young women who were asked to identify their gender *before* the test performed worse than those asked the question after.[15]

This result held true even in studies when the priming was subconscious. In another Harvard study, when 'feminine' words (like lipstick, pink or doll), were subliminally flashed unbeknownst to participants, those primed with feminine words performed worse than those primed with neutral words.[16]

Let's think about that for a moment. If the mere *idea* of identifying as a woman somehow makes us under-perform and not achieve our actual potential or capabilities, what does that say about the limiting beliefs girls and women have internalized about our gender? Think of the destructive power of these beliefs.

Consider whether unconscious gender bias may have caused you to under-perform at some point in your life. Additionally, I invite you to think about times when you may have consciously under-performed so as not to be seen as too smart or too big for your britches... especially as against your male counterparts (whether in school growing up, in the workplace, or in your intimate relationships).

(iii) Undercutting Our Own Sense of What We Think We Want

It goes even further. Not only is our *performance* negatively impacted, but some studies suggest that our very ideas about what we're even *interested in* can be manipulated by gender priming. For example, in a joint Toronto and Boston psychology study, female undergraduate students who were subliminally flashed with images of women not visible to the naked eye, expressed a preference for arts over math whereas those who had been primed with male images did not.[17]

It's a little unnerving to consider that our very choices may not be our own, but are, in fact, determined in part by unconscious biases at play.

It's for this reason that we're seeing a new burst of attention to ensuring visibility for women in STEM (Science, Technology, Engineering, Mathematics) careers to counterbalance the longtime biases that caused young women to believe they were less capable in these areas. Geena Davis's Institute on Gender in Media has done some fabulous work on increasing visibility of women in our media on the premise that *if she can see it, she can be it.*

(iv) Undercutting Our Opportunities

These unconscious biases also limit our opportunities in the world. Nowhere is that more prevalent than in the workforce. It was long believed that women did not advance or secure certain positions due to lesser skills. Allegations of bias were met with resistance and denial (from both men and women).

Now, however, studies routinely confirm that not only do these biases exist, but they've played a significant role in holding women back for many years.

In one study, for example, participants were asked to choose the most qualified candidate for a position as police chief. Unbeknownst to them, however, they were given two resumes identical in every respect but for name. One bore a man's name, the other a woman's. In significant numbers, participants (both men and women) consistently chose the male for the position notwithstanding identical resumes to choose from.[18]

Likewise, for many years, most major symphonies were overwhelmingly comprised of male musicians. Suggestions of gender bias in the selection process were rebuffed with arguments about judging by professionals based on objective, identifiable criteria. And yet, when blind audition tests were finally run (i.e., the judges could not see the candidates auditioning but could only hear them) more women were selected.[19]

This unequal access to opportunity continues up the food chain. There was much hoopla about the rise of women CEOs in Fortune 500 companies recently. In 2020, *Forbes* ran an article touting the increase in female CEOs given that year's 'highest representation' for women at 7.4%.[20]

For 2021, *Fortune* ran an article celebrating all-time records for female CEOs with female leadership for Fortune 500 companies hitting 8.1%.[21] Considering that over 50% of the population is women, we may want to question the celebratory fervor. While we're moving in the right direction, we clearly have a long way to go still.

We also see unequal access to funds. Adding insult to injury, it appears that we're moving in the wrong direction on this issue. Stats on venture capital funding going to women-led start-ups actually fell from 2.8% to 2.3% in 2020.[22] While both these numbers are staggering in the obvious differential treatment and access to funds as between men and women, the fact that the numbers are decreasing should give serious cause for pause. Needless to say, lack of access to funding significantly adversely impacts on women's ability to achieve parity in business.

(v) How Do We Start to Redress This Problem?

Surprised? It's not really surprising that these unconscious biases exist and have had profound impact on women throughout the years and continue to do so. Let's face it. It wasn't that long ago that women didn't have the right to vote, or own property. Heck, in some jurisdictions it's still recent history they were even recognized as persons in the eyes of the law. And if we go back further, in the scheme of things, it's not so long ago that powerful women were burned as witches at the stake.

So perhaps it's no wonder that you may have been conditioned to hesitate to step into the fullness of your power. The message that you will be cut down if you do has perhaps been passed down generation to generation through whispered warnings absorbed through osmosis as they travelled along our mother's umbilical cord, tying us to our mother and all the mothers before her.

Not only does this conditioning create resistance to stepping into our power, but it also affects our sense of self-worth. Messaging that we have less value creeps into our psyche.

Again, don't panic. Awareness is the key. Each layer we peel back gets you one step closer to stepping into your power as a negotiator.

It's important that we face it though. Don't turn away or pretend it doesn't exist. Look the monster in the face and name it. Hold up a mirror and face it in yourself. Stare it down.

Consider this a primary negotiation exercise. Negotiate with yourself to deal with *your* unconscious gender bias. Acknowledge the power it's held. Commit to fight against it. Identify it when it creeps in and stomp it down—both as it impacts on you and as against other women.

It starts with self-reflection and awareness. Until we can unapologetically own our internal value, how can we expect others to recognize it? Note I said internal value. Women have a tendency to seek their value and validation from external sources. This starts young as we seek to please (and so gain perceived increased value) from our parents, teachers, friends, etc., and continues to our romantic and professional relationships later in life. Our sense of value needs to come from inside first. We can't control how others see or value us, but we can take control of the value we ascribe to ourselves.

Do you practice unconditional self-love?
Do you have an unshakable sense
of your own inherent value and worth?

Given that both men and women suffer from these unconscious biases, it stands to reason that we've underperformed at some points in our lives, that we've made decisions informed by internal biases we weren't even aware were at play, that we've judged other women more harshly based on these same biases.

When I thought about these studies, it made me wonder, how many times have I held myself back or pursued a path that may not have been my heart's desire without being aware of it.

How about you?
Can you think of a time or times when you
underperformed and you weren't sure why, or you stopped
yourself from asking for more money, or let a man take
your idea, or held your tongue until you thought it might
bleed, or doubted yourself and held back from going for
something big?

And what about times when you held back or made yourself smaller because some part of you was worried about seeming 'too much'?

I invite you to list as many examples as you can think of where that was the case. And then I encourage you to take the antidote.

Brag on yourself! Create a 'Brag Journal'.
List as many positive attributes as you can about yourself.
Don't be shy. Don't worry about being cocky.
List your assets—physical, mental, attitude.
Things you're good at. Things you've accomplished.
Nice things other people have said about you.
Or nice things people could or should say about you.
List them all.
Keep going until your hand gets tired.
Then take a break, and list some more!

Brag. You deserve it!

Not only do you deserve it, but this exercise is valuable as a means to start retraining your brain… to offset, overcome and reprogram the conditioning discussed above.

I invite you to start your Brag Journal today. Read it each night before you go to bed, when your brain is most receptive to implant new subconscious belief systems. Add to your brag list each night and let yourself bask in a sense of your own worth as you sleep.

If you thought that was hard, I invite you to go a step further. If you'll open yourself to try, this is the really fun part.

Shoot a video of yourself being your fullest, boldest, most daring, confident self.
Don't hold back.

Bring all your 'too much-ness'
that you've been holding inside.
Dress boldly.
Dance, sing, speak–whatever moves you–
whatever would seem 'too much' to you.
Don't worry, you don't have to share if you don't want
(although I'd love it if you do).
You don't even have to save it if you don't want.
It's the doing it that's important. You can delete it
right after you've watched it if that will embolden you
to actually create your audacious video.
But if you're feeling brave, by all means share it.

Whatever you choose, have fun. Let loose. Let go of those conditioned inhibitions and let your inner goddess and natural negotiator shine bright.

III. Defining Conflict & Power

Reframing Conflict

How we define conflict is also part of the problem. Exploring dictionary definitions of conflict, the following words or phrases pop up:

- ➤ Fight
- ➤ Battle
- ➤ War
- ➤ Antagonistic state or action
- ➤ Competitive or opposing action
- ➤ Incompatible goals
- ➤ Collision
- ➤ Disagreement

➤ Clash of interest (usually over limited resources)
➤ Perceived threat
➤ Struggle

Perhaps the most unnerving was "may often have physical or psychological harm or destruction of their opponent as a goal."[23]

Really?! No wonder people have resistance to conflict!

Think about the consequences of these definitions of conflict. If we're conditioned to perceive conflict in these terms, it's no surprise that it triggers our lizard brain and with it a fight, flight or freeze response.

These definitions are also premised on a scarcity mindset, one where we assume we're fighting over limited resources. This approach invariably leads to a competitive response.

This perception is more likely to adversely impact women given our conditioning to be 'good girls', to 'play nice', to be 'givers not takers'.

Instead, I invite you to reframe conflict.

What if, instead of a scarcity mindset, we approached life with an abundance mindset? Where you didn't see life as a finite pie from which you had to clamor to get your slice, but rather, as offering unlimited resources. What if you chose to believe that there is all the love you need in this world; all the time you need; enough business for everyone; enough food for all; and yes… even enough toilet paper for all?

What if you chose to see conflict as a valuable opportunity for growth, allowing people to consider and produce new and different ideas. What if it was constructive and necessary, opening the world to alternatives, allowing increased participation and reassessment, helping to build community and cohesiveness? What if conflict was the path to resolve problems and increase tolerance of differing views and perspectives?

Imagine how different negotiations would be if you approached conflict from that mindset. If it didn't have to be about right or wrong, win or lose. Imagine what a difference that simple shift could make.

Reframing Power

Tied to defining conflict is how we define power. Conditioning around power is another problem that interferes with our ability to step into our best negotiating selves. At the heart of many conflicts is an underlying sense of powerlessness. Yet, what is power? How do we define it? How do we get it? How do we use it effectively? Sadly, there is too little thought given to these questions. We often buy into a misguided sense of what it means to have, hold, or exert power. We're encouraged (sometimes subtly, sometimes not so much so) to crave power. This is not surprising in a world where we define success based on a competitive model. Our entertainment industry even has us cheering on anti-heroes in their quest for power at any cost.

I invite you to reframe how you look at power so you can bring it to the bargaining table in more elegant and constructive ways. We've been taught to view power as power *over* others versus power *with*. In fact, the Miriam-Webster dictionary defines power as: "possession of control, authority, or influence over others" – as if we own control over others.

It's an important distinction to make. When we seek to exert power *over* others, we miss out on valuable opportunities to find creative solutions that better benefit all. By contrast, when we bring empathy to the table, truly seeking to understand and meet the needs of others, seeking to find power together (i.e. power *with* others), we can secure better outcomes, better buy-in, better relationships, and longer-lasting agreements.

I invite you to seek more positive power levers in your bargaining. Here are a few power sources you can tap into as a starting point:

➤ Power of Purpose
➤ Power of Collaboration
➤ Power of Service
➤ Power of Proximity
➤ Psychological Power

➤ Power of Expectation
➤ Role Power

**What power levers can you bring
to the table for better outcomes?
How can you increase your power in constructive ways?**

IV. Blocks

If you're not experiencing the negotiating success you'd like, at some level you're blocking that success. Raising your awareness about your own limiting beliefs and blocks is a key step to shift into the persuasive negotiator you're meant to be. By identifying and challenging your current blocks, you'll be on the road to substitute them with more empowering beliefs that will elevate your confidence... and with it your influence.

Let's explore some blocks that may be interfering with your powerful negotiating self:

(i) Negative Assumptions about Your Negotiating Abilities

Do you have negative assumptions about your ability to negotiate effectively? If so, you're not alone. As noted earlier, many women have bought into the myth that successful negotiation is a 'man's game'. Added to that, we often carry baggage based on the social conditioning problems discussed in Part II.

While this is understandable (especially in light of a history where for many generations, not only were women unable to negotiate for or hold property, they were regarded *as* property), it's critical to break free of these thoughts.

What you resist, persists.

Where your focus goes, energy flows.

Know that your words and your thoughts have power. Your thoughts, and the meaning you give them, create your reality.

If you approach negotiations telling yourself:

➤ "I'm a terrible negotiator."
➤ "I don't like negotiating because I hate conflict."
➤ "I have a hard time standing up for myself."
➤ "People take advantage of me."
➤ "I'm an easy target."
➤ "I shouldn't ask for too much or I'll look greedy."

(or any other variation of your particular brand of self-flagellating negative self-talk), how do you think you'll show up? How effective do you think you'll be in getting what you want?

Carrying negative self-beliefs is a classic form of self-sabotage. You will live into your expectations. Your brain will try to give you what it thinks you want.

I invite you to let go of the negative thoughts about your ability and instead reach for a better reality.

How do you rate your negotiating abilities?
If you believe you're not effective as a negotiator, how can
you flip the stories you've been telling yourself?

(ii) Believing You Don't Deserve

Women are more likely to judge ourselves as undeserving. Again, these limiting beliefs come from our social conditioning. At our core, we often grow up questioning our worth… questioning our value… believing that we're 'not enough'.

This is not surprising when even parents unwittingly often over-value the achievements of sons as compared to daughters. Not only are men more likely to rate themselves higher in IQ than their female counterparts, but parents are more likely to rate their sons as having higher IQ than daughters and believe their boys hit milestones earlier even in the face of objective evidence to the contrary.[24]

This inner sense of being 'less than' is exacerbated by the 'good girl' expectations. I remember first recognizing this pattern with my daughter when she yet again deferred to her two younger brothers when there were only two brownies left on the plate, saying, "It's okay, I don't want one. The boys can have them." When my husband responded by saying, "Oh, that's so sweet, Jade," he wasn't prepared for my passionate and immediate denunciation. He was left flummoxed as I ranted that there was no way Jade was going to be conditioned to believe it was her lot in life to take less or believe she deserved less than the men around her in life.

Believing that we're not enough or 'less than' stops us from asking for what we want and deserve. Not exactly great qualities for bargaining. It holds us back from achieving our full potential as negotiators. As we noted in discussing the importance of setting high aspirations, if you show up already believing you don't deserve what you're seeking, you're not likely to be particularly effective as a negotiator.

As women, we need to start owning our worth before we can fully step into our bargaining power… both personally and professionally. The Brag Journal from Part II is a good start to reclaim your power.

(iii) Resistance to Receive

Women are also conditioned from a young age to be and be seen as selfless nurturers and caregivers. We're led to believe that wanting for ourselves is inconsistent with our essence. It starts young, as evidenced by Jade and the brownie example above, and it hounds us throughout life with higher and higher consequences.

We tend to martyr ourselves, believing it's incumbent upon us to always be in the giving role, whether with our intimate partners, our kids, friends, co-workers and beyond. As a result, we resist receiving… in everything from compliments, to gifts, to accolades and our just desserts. This resistance blocks us from achieving all that could be available to us.

I was guilty of this for many years. Going out, I always insisted on picking up the tab. I'd say, "You can get it next time". But next time I'd do the same thing. I had to do the inner work necessary to identify this as a symptom of my 'resistance to receive' block before I could work on resolving it.

Not surprisingly, resistance to receiving can be a serious block to getting best negotiated outcomes. It not only makes us shy away from asking for what we want, but even makes us reluctant to take what's offered. This is not a great recipe for negotiation success.

(iv) Living in a 'One Day' Mindset

If you find yourself thinking "if or when I can just get x, then I would be …" or "when this happens, then I can …", you're in what I call a 'one day' mindset.

This is a dangerous place to be as 'one day' rarely comes. When we fall into this trap, there will always be another hurdle, another 'thing to get' or 'thing that needs to happen' before you allow yourself to go for what you want.

In negotiting with yourself to pursue your passion and purpose, maybe you'll tell yourself that you're just waiting until the kids start school. Or finish school. Or leave the house. Or you'll convince yourself you need one more degree or certificate or reference or testimonial.

In situations where you ought to advocate for yourself, you'll demure, telling yourself you're waiting until you're just a little better positioned.

I invite you to stop putting your life on hold, pushing away the abundance that awaits you, waiting for some external catalyst. Be your own catalyst.

(v) Environment

Are you surrounded by people who support your ambition and goals unconditionally? Or, even with the best of intentions, do the people in your life make you question your ability to take risks to succeed?

It's sometimes those closest to us who make us question our ability to achieve our goals. Our parents, wanting to keep us safe and/or avoid failure, can hold us back from stepping into the full force of our power. Our friends and/or romantic partners, used to seeing us in a particular role or way of being, may balk at our bold new initiatives and cause us to doubt ourselves. Our co-workers or superiors in the workplace may be conditioned to see us in our current position and not share our vision for our potential.

It's important to know your own value and have a clear sense of your worth. Additionally, it's important to manage your environment to get intentional about surrounding yourself with people who elevate you to be your most powerful self.

When I first started Women On Purpose, many of the people who I most expected to support my vision were the ones who least stepped up. It seemed risky, if not downright crazy, to them that I would be starting a new venture when I'd built a lucrative law practice. Not only did they fail to engage, encourage or promote me, but they planted seeds of doubt. Had I not had an unshakable conviction and passion for the importance of this work, those seeds would have taken root and stopped me from moving forward into my dreams.

Additionally, I had the foresight to ensure I joined Masterminds and other groups to surround myself with inspiring like-minded people to elevate my vision, encourage big asks and set high aspirations.

It's said that you're likely to be in a position that's the average of the 5 people you most spend time with. So, I invite you to take a close look at your current 'inner circle'. If it's not filled with people who uplift and inspire you to be the best possible version of you, then it's time to add some new people into your inner circle. This will give you the power of proximity discussed earlier under the Reframe Power section.

It may be time to reframe your environment to reframe your thoughts.

Do you recognize any of these blocks in your life? If so, celebrate! It means you're on your way to dissolving the blocks that have been getting in your way.

V. Fear

Women are often fearful, nervous or anxious about negotiations at some level and so they don't step into their natural feminine strength and power as a negotiator. Or, as mentioned earlier, those same fears drive other women to overcompensate, bringing masculine energy to the table that may not be authentic (and accordingly not most effective) for them.

I invite you to let go of the fear of bargaining. Fear will tank your confidence, which in turn will tank your credibility and persuasiveness.

Have you ever tried to convince a child not to be scared when you're oozing worry? It won't work.

The words we say are only a small part of our communications in bargaining. Our facial expressions (macro and micro), our body language, our tone of voice and even the energy we give off all send strong signals to the people we interact with. This holds true in our daily lives and in our negotiations.

I remember visiting my aunt as a child. She was terrified of storms. To her credit, she'd try to assure us kids there was nothing to worry about. I wasn't afraid of storms—in fact I loved them. But seeing her wide-eyed abject terror, with her lips pulled back in what she hoped was a reassuring smile, in combination with her quivering voice was enough to set the entire household on anxious high alert.

Equally important, she'd feed on her own fear, and ultimately end up shouting "Lordy, save yourselves, get under the beds!" as her Newfie roots kicked in and she clamored to scramble under the closest bed in the wake of a thunderclap.

Admittedly Aunt Minnie is an extreme example, and it's a funny story today, but there are lessons there. Her fear did not inspire confidence. It was easy to take advantage of her in that state (as my cousins can attest). She lost all clarity and was unable to meet her objectives. She fed on her own fear, undermining her own confidence and capabilities. She lost out on opportunities.

All of these consequences apply equally when you approach your negotiations from a place of fear. Succumbing to fear will almost always detract from your effectiveness, in bargaining and in life.

When you approach negotiations with fear, you undermine your effectiveness (both internally and externally) before you even get a chance to convey your message. Others will feel it and use it. You'll feel it and if unchecked or unmanaged it will feed on you and suck your comfort, confidence and competence.

Fear typically also drops your energy and ability to maintain clarity. It should come as no surprise that maintaining clarity in bargaining is critical.

As a practical matter, fear also tends to make us too chatty. Talking too much is a vice in negotiations. You will likely give up information, to your detriment. Contrary to popular belief, the more someone talks in bargaining, the less confident they are about their position.

Perception is important. Both for those you deal with, and internally, for yourself. Visualization exercises are valuable for this reason. What we think, we become. If we approach negotiations from a place of fear, we will be calling that which we fear.

By contrast, when we approach negotiations from a place of confidence, we exude certainty, build rapport and trust, and are more likely to manifest what we seek.

Now that you recognize the urgency of facing your fears to up-level your skill as a negotiator, let's explore some of the most popular fear factors and why you want to avoid them in your bargaining to ensure you get what you want and deserve.

(i) Fear of Failure

Under-achievers and over-achievers alike often suffer from fear of failure. You may think of it as fear of embarrassment, fear of rejection, or fear of being judged. It manifests in a number of ways and tells. People you negotiate with can feel this fear which weakens your position vis-à-vis them.

Fear of failure typically either has us step back and away from our power, or alternatively, overcompensate in an attempt to cover it with whitewash. Neither approach serves the higher negotiator in you.

For some, this fear stems from a mistaken belief that your personal worth will be defined by the outcome of the negotiation. That if you *get* less in your negotiation it will mean you *are* less. This is why the inner work is so important and why I spend so much time on this with my coaching clients.

You need to develop an unshakable sense of self. Practice unconditional self-love. Determine your internal value and own it. When you build that confidence, you won't define your self worth based on the results you achieve (or don't) in any isolated negotiation.

Ironically, in fearing failure you call it to you. Focusing on failure distracts you from your real outcome, compromises your clarity, diminishes your communication, and undermines your comfort and confidence. You'll lose sight of your compelling vision for the future and pull back. Or at the other end, you'll get too chatty. The more you talk, the more ammunition you give and the *less* command you'll hold.

This fear also keeps us small as we tend to stay boxed in our comfort zone, resistant to trying anything that may lead to perceived failure. We're less likely to take the kinds of risks that lead to better negotiation outcomes.

I invite you to dig deep to determine the real source of this fear. Usually something else underlies fear of failure and when you can name it, you can fight it, or better yet, learn to use it to fuel you.

For a hot tip on how to deal with fear of failure, see 'Reframe Failure' in Fast Track Inner Work Tips. This is an area where you can make powerful shifts.

(ii) Fear of Success

The oft-ignored sister to fear of failure, is fear of success. We often subconsciously fear and shrink away from the full strength of our power. This is particularly true for women. Limiting beliefs that likely dogged us since childhood hold us back. These are often tied to baggage around money/wealth (rich people are greedy and money is the root of all evil); our sense of worth (I'm not enough); being seen (I'll be judged or shunned if I'm seen as 'too much'); and/or tall poppy syndrome (if I stand out, I'll be cut down).

Based on these debilitating beliefs, we self-sabotage and prevent ourselves from achieving the full level of success or power that could be within our grasp. And so, it's important to do the inner work on these internal limiting beliefs if you want to be your most effective negotiator. Why not reframe your fear and use it as a source of empowerment?

I particularly love Marianne Williamson's quote on this issue:

Our greatest fear is not that we are inadequate, but that we are powerful beyond measure. It is our light, not our darkness that brightens us. We ask ourselves 'who am I to be brilliant, gorgeous, handsome, talented and fabulous?' Actually, who are you not to be?… Your playing small does not serve the world. There is nothing enlightened about shrinking so that other people won't feel insecure around you.

I unwittingly suffered from fear of success for a long time. Coming from a low-income background, I carried a lot of unconscious judgment about money and people with money. There were many arguments about cash growing up—there just never seemed to be enough. I remember sitting around our tiny Formica kitchen table in our tiny apartment, listening to my dad talk about 'the rich'. I learned to equate money with want at one end and greed or exploitation at the other.

And so, it's perhaps no surprise that as my law practice thrived, I always felt the need to justify any perceived extravagances or successes. When I got my first 'luxury' vehicle, a Cadillac Escalade, I was so self-conscious about it that I'd drive around a hearing venue to park in the back if I happened to see clients out front. I was embarrassed to be seen in my 'fancy ride'. I feared being judged, and at a deeper level, I was concerned about the impact it might have on my relationships with my working-class client base.

This thinking kept me small. It stopped me from charging what I was worth. It blocked me from bigger deals and opportunities. I got great results for my clients but sabotaged myself from catapulting to the next level until I was able to recognize and push past this fear.

Get ruthlessly honest with yourself. Ask yourself what aspects of success scare you.

Is there a relationship you're afraid might change or be impacted by your success?

Are you afraid you'll give up your sense of self or your identity if you become too successful?

Are you afraid of how you may be judged by others in your life if you become one of '*them*'?

Recognizing your fears around success is the first step in allowing you to change the stories you've been telling yourself that keep you plateauing… or worse.

(iii) Fear of Losing

This fear stems from a belief that negotiation is about winning or losing. Approaching negotiations with this mindset sets you behind the eight ball from the outset.

Effective negotiation is about securing your outcome, not beating the other party. What if you shifted your mindset so that 'winning' any given negotiation was no longer your objective? Instead, what if your goal was simply to achieve your desired outcome (or better yet, to find a better outcome for all parties)?

When you focus on beating the other party (or looking good), you lose the clarity and focus required for effective bargaining. You may lose sight of alternatives and opportunities and sacrifice your desired outcome by focusing on a perceived 'win' over the other side. You've no doubt heard the expression, 'win the battle to lose the war'. Sometimes in bargaining, you need to be open to concede certain points with a view to securing a better ultimate end result.

I remember many years ago, bargaining with counsel who was notorious for personalizing the process. He'd often attack opposing counsel and routinely try to undermine them in front of the adjudicator or client. Sure enough, he lived up to his reputation, and immediately started jousting for the upper hand. I confess, that my younger self at first took the bait, and became focused on winning the argument at hand. As we each dug in and costly litigation seemed certain, it suddenly struck me that I could give him what he was asking for while putting my client in an even better position than they'd originally been seeking. I was able to turn his desire to 'win' against him to secure an even better overall result by returning my focus to the outcome over the so-called 'win'.

Or perhaps, more than a desire to win, counsel was driven by a desire not to lose. Interestingly, studies show that psychologically, people are more driven *not to lose* than they are *to win*. As a result, smart negotiators will always look beyond the hard candy exterior of the other party and pay attention to the soft candy center they are trying to protect. When you can hone in on what loss the other person is trying to avoid, you can better tailor your strategy toward approaches that get what you need while steering clear of the perceived loss for them. Always leave the other party a way out or way to walk away (or buy in) with dignity.

[This resistance to loss is discussed under the Bias section: Loss Aversion Bias.]

(iv) Fear of Missing Out (FOMO)

Do you suffer from FOMO (fear of missing out)? Do you worry that you're going to be left behind or miss a great opportunity? High-pressure sales-people bank on this human fear. They create urgency and a sense of scarcity to push for a quick close based on quick-fix or get-rich-fast desires. They prey on fear of missing out.

The same holds true in other forms of bargaining. Beware of artificially imposed time constraints or promises of rare, limited opportunities. Think twice if you're being deprived of the chance to do your due diligence. If it seems too good to be true, it usually is.

I've been guilty of this. I remember being lured into the attraction of a 'guaranteed' quick turnaround stock option. A friend called with a hot tip, sure-thing opportunity, but I had no opportunity for due diligence—I had to buy it right then. I did. I lost every penny.

Fear of missing out is also often used as a bargaining tactic where the other party plays to your need to belong or keep up with the proverbial

'Jones'. In our competitive, comparative approach to life we can easily fall prey to suggestions that 'everyone is doing it' or getting it. We fear being left on the outside looking in.

Be mindful of this tactic and aware of your own susceptibility to fear falling on the short end of a self-imposed comparison. I mean really, has anyone ever met this perfect 'Jones' family that we torture ourself with in our imaginary comparing?

(v) Fear of the Unknown

Were you afraid of the dark as a kid? Does the thought of venturing into a new situation or deal, without all the facts, make you break out in a sweat? If things are moving too quickly in a negotiation (or life situation) and you have unanswered questions about all the possible implications or permutations of what you're contemplating, are you likely to walk away altogether?

Fear of the unknown can paralyze us from moving forward. While preparation is a good thing, sometimes we can get bogged down in the paralysis of analysis and miss valuable opportunities. I've seen many a good deal die or nearly get scuttled by one party's need to try to pin down every possible eventuality that may come to pass.

This is where your preparation is key. Ensure you have clarity about the outcomes you seek. If you're someone who hates uncertainty, consider (in advance of the negotiation) all the possible things that could go wrong. Then determine how you would handle it if any of these scenarios came to pass. Usually, you'll find that contemplating it in advance takes the edge off, as it's the fear of the unknown that really drives your resistance. Once you've addressed it head on, it loses its power. Or alternatively, for those few things that you really couldn't tolerate, you can build protections into the deal or walk away if they're not addressed.

At the other end of the spectrum, are you the type to dive off the cliff, asking how deep the water is on the way down? If so, you will inevitably be dealing with someone who fits in the above category at some point. It will no doubt frustrate you to no end fielding the seemingly never-ending barrage of questions that you see as unnecessary overkill. Recognizing their fear of the unknown allows you to address their concerns proactively to avoid losing the deal.

(vi) Fear of Being Seen as a B*t#h

Under the 'Problems' section of this book (Keeping Ourselves Small) we discussed the impact of social conditioning on women. Specifically, how we grow to fear being seen as 'too much' and so keep ourselves small. This self-sabotage extends to a general fear of being judged. To be fair, there is some basis for that.

Studies show that both men and women tend to judge successful women more harshly. Where participants were shown identical pictures of a boardroom table save for who sat at the head of the table—in one photo a man headed the table whereas the other photo depicted a woman at the head spot—when asked to describe the person at the head of the table, the man was routinely described in very complimentary terms (i.e., strong, leader, charismatic, etc.) whereas the woman was described in less complimentary terms (i.e., overbearing, controlling, arrogant, etc.).[25] Note that these reactions were consistent across the gender divide. In other words, both male and female participants judged the woman more harshly.

In a similar themed study out of Columbia Business School, students were given identical stories to read with only one difference. One story had the rags to riches protagonist named Heidi, the other Howard. Again, both the male and female student participants, when asked to comment on the likability of the main character, found the male character to be a hero but the female lead to be difficult and unlikable—based on identical stories but for their gender.[26]

And so, it's perhaps no surprise that women tend to believe they need to 'play nice' so as not to be judged by their peers. Yet the more women buy into this practice, the more we perpetuate the problem.

Think of the example you set for other young women when you shy away from your power and potential, when you step back from opportunities for fear of how you may be perceived by others without any foundation whatsoever. We give credibility to the baseless myths and preserve the problematic patterns.

The antidote to this fear of judgment is twofold.

(I) Call out the baseless judgments—for yourself and others. Be vigilant of your own internal conditioned biases and catch yourself in the act. Call out others you see falling prey to this precedent. Much like negotiating tactics, when we call them out, they lose their power.

(II) Get intentional about redefining your sense of self-worth and value.

As Eleanor Roosevelt said, "No one can make you feel inferior without your consent."

Banish your inner critic. Shut down your self-doubter. Practice positive self-talk—always. Decide who you want to be - who you want to show up as. Envision it. Believe it. See yourself as already embodying that version of you.

As Buddha said, "What you think, you become. What you feel, you attract. What you imagine, you create."

Your thoughts have power. The good news is that you control your thoughts.

These are just a few of the fears that hold us back in bargaining.

Do any of these fears resonate with you?
What's your fear-poison?

It's important to recognize your fears and name them. Identifying the fear is half the battle in overcoming its power in your negotiations.

Consider what fears first come to mind. Then determine if your first thought is, in fact, superficial, and if a deeper fear is at play. Perhaps your fear of failure is really a fear of success at its root. Dig deep. Truly seeing your fears and their impact is a key first step to letting them go or being able to use them to propel you to the next level.

Conscious awareness of your fears will give you more control, ease, clarity, confidence and perspective—all of which will help you keep your eye on the outcome to increase your chances of getting what you want or more in your bargaining and your life. Learning to identify and name your fears will start you on a journey of empowerment where you'll be able to use your fears to propel you in bargaining and beyond.

Think of the Boggart from the *Harry Potter* series. The Boggart was a shapeshifting being that took the form of its observer's worst fear. Professor Lupin had the young wizards and witches face-off against the Boggart, forcing them to confront their worst fears and banish them with the Riddikulus (ridiculous) spell.

**Try the Boggart exercise with your worst fear.
Name it. Face it. Banish it.**

From CEO's, to entrepreneurs or those in life transitions, whether established or starting, my clients have all seen great success by facing and overcoming these fears. They become better leaders as CEO's, business owners, politicians and beyond. They make significantly greater sales (with ease) as entrepreneurs and for those who provide services, they confidently charge more for their services when they crack these barriers.

The impact in their personal lives is also profound as they release the fears that bring baggage to their relationships and historically caused them to show up as lesser versions of themselves.

Reframing your fear can be another powerful tool. You can use the fear to fuel you rather than shrink from it. Some physiological responses to fear are twin versions of more empowering states. Nervousness, for example, is the twin sister to excitement. You can use this knowledge to flip the fear story you tell yourself to a more powerful one.

I remember backstage in the green room, before my TEDx talk (*Rise of the Feminine Voice as the Key to Our Future*), I was surprised to find myself nervous. I love public speaking and I've always thrived on the energy of a crowd. I never got butterflies. I couldn't figure what was happening as my stomach did loop-de-loops and I was sure I'd forget half my talk and the words would elude me. Before full-blown panic set in I got a grip on myself, took a couple deep breaths, banished the idea that I was *nervous* and instead reminded myself that I was *excited* for the opportunity to share this subject I was so passionate about. That subtle shift totally changed my perspective and my ability to show up from a place of power.

Letting go of the fear, reframing it, or at least recognizing how to give it a backseat will increase your persuasiveness and your results along with it.

As always, the flip-side of this coin is key as well. Once you've identified and mastered your own potential fears in advance of a negotiation, turn your mind to the likely fears that may dog the other party. Bring that empathy to the table. Understanding blocks that may stand in their way and considering what impact those fears could have and how you might best address it will make you a more effective negotiator.

YOUR SECRET WEAPONS

I. What Are Your Secret Weapons?

After hearing about the problems, no doubt you're ready to hear some good news. Well, here it is. As women, we have secret weapons in our negotiating arsenal.

The first secret weapon is simply this. People don't expect you to be effective as a negotiator. This holds true, not only for men but for women too. Being under-estimated can position you to get better outcomes while flying under the radar.

Tied to that, the second secret weapon is that people assume negotiation is all about the bark and bite. This is one of the key reasons that most people (both men and women) assume that women aren't as effective as negotiators. And they're simply wrong. Knowing that is a key advantage in negotiations.

If the thought of getting 'assertive' makes you break out in a sweat, don't panic. I've got your back. In fact, of the six key markers of a highly effective negotiator, at least five of the six traits are typically considered 'feminine'. Learning to be intentional in invoking these traits is a huge advantage in negotiations.

Together, we're going to explore those six key elements and break them down to demystify the concept of negotiation. You'll learn how to use your natural skills to be a highly effective negotiator.

II. What are the 6 Key Skillsets of Effective Negotiators?

Let's jump right in to explore the most widely recognized skills you need to be a powerhouse negotiator.

➤ Assertiveness
➤ Rapport-building
➤ Empathy
➤ Flexibility
➤ Intuition
➤ Trustworthiness

Here's a handy mnemonic to help you remember them: ARE FIT

Just think: You ARE FIT to be a great negotiator.

You already use these skills every day. Learning to use them with intention is a powerful secret weapon.

A - Assertiveness

This is the only negotiation skill of our ARE FIT sextuplet that is considered by many to be a more 'masculine' trait. The expectation is that women will be less assertive in bargaining. In fact, this is the main reason the myth that women are not effective negotiators was born. The doubly mistaken beliefs that (i) toughness carries the day in bargaining and (ii) women shy away from toughness, have caused both men and women to believe women aren't as effective in the negotiation arena.

In fact, however, as noted above, toughness does not necessarily carry the day. Assertiveness is only one of six key skills routinely brought to bear by the most effective negotiators. Negotiators who are adept at bringing rapport-building, empathy, flexibility, intuition and trust to the table can routinely trump someone whose only go-to is assertiveness.

Further, it's not true that women can't be assertive. Just ask anyone who's ever had to deal with a mother protecting her child or other loved one. While some women shy away from advocating strongly for themselves, most women are unequivocally effective when advocating for someone else, particularly someone they care about. The fact that women can bring assertiveness to the table when advocating for others reinforces that women do have this skill. We just need to tap into it more regularly.

It should also be noted that assertiveness is typically considered a masculine trait based on a misconception where people conflate assertive with aggressive. They are not the same thing. Assertive does not mean being tough for the sake of being tough. It doesn't mean table-pounding, chest-beating, shouting, belittling, attacking or any other misguided sense of boldness or forcefulness. It means being confident and self-assured, holding the line when required. That confidence comes, in part, from knowledge, which comes from putting the work in and being prepared.

> *Assertiveness comes from confidence.*
> *Confidence comes from knowledge.*
> *Knowledge comes from preparation.*

In fact, forty-five percent (45%) of bargaining success is attributed to effective preparation.

You can do that with your eyes closed. You already do it every day in a multitude of ways. And rest assured, we'll be exploring elements of effective preparation throughout this book so you'll be even more skilled in this area and even better equipped to step into your assertiveness in bargaining.

You can still be assertive while being diplomatic. As Winston Churchill famously quipped, "Diplomacy is the art of telling people to go to hell in a way that they ask for directions."

Even after I retired my 'Barracuda' moniker in favor of the more collaborative approach of HERsuasion™, nobody would ever accuse me of being a pushover. I was still able to consistently bring assertiveness to the table using the Art of Feminine Negotiation™. And the beauty was that I was able to get even better outcomes—for myself and the other parties—without the high cost of a competitive or aggressive approach.

**How would you rate your ability
to be assertive in your negotiations?**

R – Rapport-Building

Rapport-building is all about relationship. Women were required to develop this skill in a world where for too long they had so few rights. Our very survival depended on becoming adept at developing relationships. So, it's no surprise that women often show superior skill in this area and that rapport-building is typically regarded as a feminine trait or skill.

Rapport-building is all about making (rather than breaking) connection, building (rather than tearing down) bridges. It involves communication skills, seeking to find affinity, common understanding, common ground. Developing this skill involves a combination of factors including empathy, intuition, active listening, flexibility, collaboration, trustworthiness and an ability to shelve ego when needed.

This skill is important as we tend to be drawn to people who are similar to us and fear those who are different. Building rapport builds connection and a perceived shared frame of reference. It diffuses potential tension and opens lines of communication. As a result, this approach leads to increased cooperation, which in turn increases creativity, which results in better negotiated results, with greater buy-in, satisfaction and longevity. The stronger the relationship, the higher the trust and the more likely mutual ground will be found.

Some people seem able to instantly connect with others. They can build trust and connection with ease. If you're one of those people, you're positioned to be a highly effective negotiator. If not, don't fret. Contrary to popular belief, rapport-building is not an elusive gift you're either born with or destined to do without forever.

Also note that rapport can be instantaneous or it can take time to develop. It can grow naturally or you can build it with intention. Ideally, you want to both build rapport and stimulate it.

There are many ways to build rapport in a negotiation. Let's first unpack some of the foundational elements for setting the stage to build rapport and then consider some specific strategies for rapport-building as the negotiation progresses.

Be Yourself

Oscar Wilde is oft-quoted for his quip, "Be yourself—everyone else is taken."

Sage advice that still holds… in life generally and in rapport-building for negotiations in particular. Being real and authentic will always be more effective than trying to adopt a persona that isn't natural for you. The other party will feel the lack of authenticity and it will create a discord that repels rapport and trust.

There are many resources available now on how to negotiate more effectively and much written about tactics to build rapport. Studying these will certainly help elevate your skillset and improve your negotiation skills and outcomes. Having said that, don't fall into the trap of getting stuck in your head, over-thinking the 'how' and in the process losing your natural authentic charisma. Practice the skills to build rapport (including those set out here), but always err on the side of being yourself as you work towards the new skills becoming natural.

Make a Good First Impression

First impressions matter. Most people have a visceral reaction to others within seconds of meeting. Make sure the reaction you induce is positive to the extent possible. Take note of your state before you start the negotiation. Release any negativity you may be harboring. Tap into a memory or thought that puts you in a positive frame. Once you get in the desired state, it will be easier to show up with a genuine smile, with warmth in your eyes, and an inviting posture and demeanor. This will help set the stage for rapport-building right out of the gate.

As you scan your state in advance of the negotiation, remember that negativity includes nervousness, angst and uncertainty around the negotiation. Showing up without having healed these states will create a disconnect and break rapport from the outset. Ideally you want to show up with the confidence that comes from being prepared.

Note that you need to be aware of cultural sensitivities, both in making a first impression and throughout the negotiation. Ensure that you are culturally appropriate so as not to offend and break rapport.

Find Common Ground

We often hear the advice to start with small-talk. While it's true that you want to avoid jumping straight to business (which definitely does not build rapport), I'm not talking about leading with banal conversation about the weather. Try to find a common interest or connection. Maybe a shared hobby, favourite sport or team, college, travel experience, etc. Most people like talking about themselves. Show genuine interest to inspire them to open up. In so doing you will build connection and rapport.

Ideally, you want to find your shared humanity. Try to discover what brings them joy and what they're passionate about. Tapping into that will increase your ability to build rapport.

Get Curious

Tied to finding common ground, it's useful to stay curious. We all seek to be seen, heard and understood. The more you ask open questions and stay genuinely engaged, the higher the connection you'll build (not to mention the valuable information you can elicit to better understand the real needs of the other party to come up with creative higher value solutions). Ask some variation of 'tell me about yourself'.

It goes without saying that to do this effectively, you'll need to release judgment and let go of stereotypes and preconceived ideas (about the person and their position). Approaching a negotiation from a place of fascination about the other party and their position is a powerful way to build rapport.

Give a Compliment

A genuine compliment can go a long way. Find something you can truly acknowledge that you appreciate about the other person and share that.

Use the Person's Name

Try to remember and use people's names. Call them by name early in the conversation. Again, people like to be seen. Calling them by name creates an immediate connection and familiarity.

Having said that don't repeat their name so often that it stands out and jars. My husband, a small-town boy, uses people's names repeatedly in his conversations. While it's genuine and authentic for him, overuse of someone's name is risky as it comes across as insincere and can actually undermine rapport rather than build it. I often find myself wanting to kick him under the table when he's used someone's name multiple times within a few minutes of speaking.

And a word to the wise: be sure you have the person's correct name. Nothing breaks rapport like mispronouncing someone's name, or worse yet, calling them by the wrong name.

Be Candid

If you want to build rapport and trust, always be the person who tells the truth. Admit when you don't know the answer to something. Likewise, admit if you've made a mistake. We mistakenly assume this undermines our credibility when, in fact, the opposite is true. It humanizes us and makes us more relatable and trustworthy. Being honest builds rapport and a reputation for integrity.

Create Shared Experiences

If possible, try to spend time together (preferably in person) and create shared experiences outside of the negotiation process. This can turbo-charge the connection process. This doesn't mean you have to engage in a high ropes challenge or white-water-rafting adventure (as seem popular in today's team building culture) but find some activity with potential to create meaningful connection.

Mirror & Match

Be intentional about your body language and facial expressions. Maintain eye contact. Lean in slightly. Nod periodically. Where appropriate, try to mirror and match the other person. Be careful though about the popular advice today to mimic the other party (i.e., to cross your legs or arms etc. if they do). Be discreet. Unless you're skilled at mirroring, this can be obvious and jarring and actually break rapport and trust.

Rather, note their speech patterns—tone, tempo and volume—and try to match it. I tend to speak with passion, excitement, speed and volume. When speaking with someone who is more reserved, this can be off-putting and challenge rapport-building. I get intentional about slowing down my speech, toning down my volume and matching the other person's style in those cases. I also pay attention to their language choices to use terminology and idiom that is familiar to them and will be more likely to resonate. You can even repeat back the key words of their communication as they talk so the language will feel familiar for them.

Gradually Increase Intimacy

While you don't want to prematurely over-share and dump inappropriate private information, it can be powerful to gradually increase intimacy through strategic sharing of personal info. The New York Times did a poll that found people trusted 70% of those people they knew versus only 30% of those they didn't know. The more you can create a personal connection, where they feel they know you, and get comfortable sharing with you, the more likely you are to build the bond and rapport necessary for superior negotiated outcomes.

Inject Humor

Humor is a great antidote and connection-builder. In addition to smiling, use humor where possible. Laughter releases endorphins (our feel-good chemicals in the body) and relaxes us. This sets the mood and opens the way for better bonding.

If you lose rapport at any point in a negotiation, don't ignore the elephant in the room. Be humble. Address why you lost rapport. Take ownership where appropriate. Apologize if necessary. Get curious and determine together how you can get back on track.

How many of these strategies have you typically used to create rapport in your negotiations?

Practice and get comfortable with these approaches so they become natural and you can slip into rapport-building mode authentically. Building better relationships will get you better negotiated outcomes.

E - Empathy

Tied to rapport-building (to the extent that it's a skill which enhances rapport) is empathy. Empathy is the art of being able to put yourself in the shoes of another person, the capacity to understand another's feelings from their frame of reference, to show compassion, sympathy, concern, and consideration. This skill has long been regarded as a 'feminine' quality. Truly understanding the other party's perspective and motivation is a powerful tool in any negotiation.

Imagine the strategic power that comes from anticipating the other party's needs and desires, to see where your counterpart is coming from and to understand their emotions even (or especially) when you don't agree. It allows you to better frame your positions with a tailored view to addressing or avoiding both positive and negative potential triggers, to determine where to best give or take, when to push or pull back, and how to present to increase your odds of getting what you want and need.

Understanding the motivations and triggers of the other party positions you to persuade on their own terms. It can inform what to best say and how to best say it. Not only does it give you a strategic advantage, but it also creates more receptivity and better buy-in from the other party, which will profoundly positively impact on your negotiations and the negotiated results.

Empathy can also kick-start increased creativity in the negotiation process, allowing the parties to seek and discover joint interests and creative win-win solutions. It is also more likely to trigger acknowledgements of mistakes, a trait which can give traction in negotiations.

Note that having empathy for another's position does not mean you necessarily agree. This is a common misconception and often gets in the way of a resolution. When you resist the other person's position because you fear being seen to agree, you aren't likely to build the requisite trust as you won't bring empathy to the table. Without empathy, you're less likely to have meaningful dialogue, which means you're less likely to come up with best solutions. The U.S. political polarization is a great example of this as was the global polarization around COVID best practices. There was little meaningful open discourse and as a result valuable opportunities for more creative and fruitful discussions and outcomes were lost.

Bringing empathy can be difficult in a negotiation where you find the other party particularly reprehensible. If someone is antagonistic, short-tempered, bullying or trying to exert power over you, you may be tempted to respond in kind. It can be challenging to put yourself in their position and seek to understand their point of view.

But we never know what someone is going through in their life. All of us, at some point, are guilty of showing up as lesser versions of ourselves. I have no doubt that going through menopause, I was not always my most cooperative self. Or, as I dealt with the pain of discovering a serious mental health issue with one of my children while simultaneously coping with the agonizing process of placing my mom in a long-term care facility, I'm quite sure there were days when I was less than a gracious bargaining counterpart.

We can weigh down negotiations with our false assumptions. As pop-star, Amanda Marshall, sang, "Everybody's got a story that could break your heart." Try to imagine that story. Envision the goodness in that person to call on your empathy.

What you resist, persists. That is why empathy is such a powerful tool. It breaks the resistance. It creates an opening. It allows space for resolution.

This is especially so when you're able to name the fear, concern or pain point of the other party. Naming (or labelling) it aloud acknowledges and validates how the other party is feeling. It takes the emotional charge out of it and allows room for rational discussion. Giving voice to it is a bridge between you and them and where you need to go.

This is a valuable skill to bring to bear in bargaining, and one that you no doubt employ on a daily basis in your life already. Empathy is increasingly being recognized as a crucial skill for success in life generally and in negotiations. In fact, this is perhaps the skill in negotiation most written about after assertiveness and yet women's seeming advantage in this skill is typically underplayed. Women are usually seen as having an advantage in virtually all the above-noted perks of empathy. We recognize this trait in our lives generally, yet most of us don't credit ourselves with this skill in the context of assessing our negotiating abilities. Isn't it past time you changed that skewed perspective and recognized your inherent strength in this key area?

Do you genuinely try to understand and meet the needs of other party in your negotiations, both personally and professionally?

F – Flexibility

The ability to be flexible—able to change, pivot or bend as necessary—is important to both the process and outcome of any given negotiation.

Process flexibility is the ability to shift styles or approaches as needed to get what you want out of the negotiation. In other words, if an assertive approach is not getting you the traction you hoped for, you can seamlessly switch to a collaborative approach (or whatever other approach you see as better fitting the particular negotiation or party).

Process flexibility also includes being flexible as to the actual 'process' of the negotiation (i.e., whether interest-based (integrative) or positional (distributive), where and when bargaining takes place, whether you sign off on articles as you go, whether you exchange proposals, etc.).

Outcome flexibility is more end-result/solution focused (i.e., the 'what', matter or substance of the negotiations). Effective negotiators will be able to find different and creative ways to meet their interests. Negotiators who come to the table with tunnel vision re outcomes, lose out on valuable opportunities to find more creative (and better) solutions than anticipated.

A fixed mind re outcome expectations can also lead to attachment where you bargain past the point when a deal makes sense for you or alternatively walk away even where a solution is lying on the table between you if you were just open to see it (discussed under 7 Deadly Sins of Negotiating).

Flexibility is typically an area where women excel. Some would say this is out of necessity. The nature of our often-harried existence (the need to juggle many balls at the same time, to multi-task in multiple areas, and to manoeuvre through the many minefields that come with being a woman) makes us well-equipped to bring flexible approaches to life and negotiations and to adapt as may be required in any given situation.

Do you typically seek, with intention, to bring and maintain flexibility in your negotiations?

I - Intuition

Being able to rely on strong instinct, to pick up on cues (both verbal and non-verbal) and to read your counterpart in negotiations is a valuable tool. These cues include non-verbal factors like eye contact, body language, tone of voice, pace, and verbal factors like use of humor or other tactics to build connection. Women are usually rated high based on these factors (and in fact, higher than men).[27] Specifically, women tend to be more effective at reading mood, body language, and tone and they also tend to give non-verbal cues that they are listening to their counterpart. This connectedness between negotiators is important to build trust.

In our fast-paced world, decisions often need to be made quickly. Negotiations are no exception. There may be little time for fulsome deliberation and judgments may need to be made with incomplete information. Intuition is key in these cases. In fact, some experts recommend building time into any negotiation to allow intuitive reflection before decision-making.

A study out of the University of Amsterdam found that participants having to decide between multiple proposals made better decisions when they put aside the proposals in question and took time to do a puzzle and follow their intuition for the final decision phase.[28] Our unconscious thought process is less restrictive than our deliberate thought processes. That's not to say that intuition should be substituted in place of preparation, but ignoring the role (and value) of intuition is a mistake.

Intuition is typically considered a feminine trait. It's called 'women's intuition' for a reason. Whether you accept that these things can be gender-based or not, it's interesting that people buy into the concept of 'women's intuition' and yet dismiss this value when assessing women's effectiveness as negotiators. I invite you to recognize, honor and celebrate your innate and developed skill in this area.

How often do you trust your intuition in your negotiations?

T - Trustworthiness

Trust is a cornerstone of effective negotiations. From trusting yourself (and your intuition), to building trust with the other party or parties, the bottom line is that trust gets better long-term outcomes, relationships, and buy-in. Yet we typically don't include intentional trust-building as an element of our preparation work for negotiations. That failure adversely impacts your ability to influence and persuade—in other words your effectiveness as a negotiator.

Your reputation and trustworthiness are key in negotiations. This is especially so for long-term bargaining relationships (whether personal or professional). Justified or not, the reality is that people tend to trust women more. Perhaps because we've not been regarded as threats, either physically and/or given our lack of historic power in business or politics. Perhaps because women are typically considered to be more open with their emotions which is perceived as transparency and candor. Perhaps it's the perception that women are more likely to ensure everyone's voices are heard. Someone suggested to me recently that it's because women are seen as mothers, nurturers, and caregivers. Whatever the rationale, the result is that it typically translates to increased innate trust, which is a definite asset in any negotiation.

For a long time, experts couldn't agree on how to define trust let alone how to actively build it. There were widely divergent opinions, across multiple disciplines, on the causes of trust, its nature, and its impact. Everyone seemed to agree it was important, but nobody could agree on why or how.

A 1995 journal article, *An Integrative Model of Organizational Trust*, spoke to the issue and is often cited for its breakdown of the factors of 'trustworthiness'.[29] They suggested that we decide whether we find someone to be trustworthy based on our assessment of the following three factors:

➤ Ability: Do I believe the person has the ability to deliver on their promises?
➤ Benevolence: Is the person inclined or motivated to do right by me?
➤ Integrity: Does the person share values and principles that are acceptable to me?

Over a decade later, drawing on the ABI model, Stephen Covey spoke to the question of trust, breaking it down to two component parts: (i) character and (ii) competence.[30] Character reflected integrity and intent. Competence drew on capabilities and results.

Would you pass the 'trust' test based on these qualities?

It's worth asking ourselves this question periodically… and in advance of every negotiation.

As noted earlier, in our fast-paced world decisions get made quickly. These speed-date decisions are often based on knee-jerk check-ins about whether we trust the other party or not. Those reflex reactions are typically based on past experiences, reputation, cues (verbal and non-verbal), etc.

Here are some hot, practical, tips on how to build trust in your negotiations:

Trust Yourself

As noted earlier, our first and most important negotiation is always negotiating our own mindset. It's difficult to build trust with others if you don't trust yourself. Do the inner work necessary to bring the confidence that comes from self-love to the table. You need to respect yourself to attract the respect of others. Explore the limiting beliefs that have held you back, challenge your inner critic, seek internal validation (versus external), be honest with yourself and celebrate your value.

Maintain Your Reputation

Losing trust is easier than building it. If you've lost someone's trust, it can take considerable investment to regain it. Managing your reputation is key. Being known as someone who is untrustworthy can be the kiss of death in negotiations. So always guard your reputation.

We sometimes assume that a particular deal is a one-off, that we won't see the person again, so we don't need to be our best self. This is a mistake. As I've matured, I appreciate more and more that it truly is a small world, and the 6 degrees of separation rule applies. It is often the case that we end up negotiating with or being impacted by people we never thought we'd see again. Maybe you (or they) changed positions, cities, careers. Or they may know someone in your circle and your reputation will precede you.

Sometimes you'll know this has happened, but often you won't. You'll be negotiating with someone who doesn't trust you from the get-go (based on reputation you built from a prior negotiation with someone you thought you'd never see again) and you're not even aware of the adverse dynamic at play. People hold on to resentments, storing them like chipmunks stockpile their proverbial winter nuts.

If you're intentional about always showing up with integrity and guarding your reputation, you'll be known as someone people want to deal with … and trust.

Give Respect

Respect and trust are closely connected. Respect breeds respect. Always treat people with dignity and respect if you expect the same. Doing so builds trust.

Bring Empathy to the Table

Be sure to practice active listening. Seek to truly understand the position and needs of the other party. This serves to lower defenses and increase the trust factor.

[See the section on Elevated Active Listening under Part IV of the 7 Deadly Sins of Negotiation for the secret sauce to this skill.]

Speak Clearly

By that, I don't mean avoid mumbling. I'm talking about being clear about your meaning—say what you mean and mean what you say. Be transparent and open where possible.

Tied to that, speak the 'language' of the other party. I'm not talking about learning the mother tongue of the other party, but rather, use the lingo and terminology that speaks to them.

As an attorney, I quickly learned to brush up on the technical or specialized lingo of my clients in order to build the requisite trust that I was able to properly represent their interests. It made clients in the trucking industry nervous if their counsel didn't know the difference between a truck tractor and a flatbed.

Make & Label Your Concessions

Be prepared to make concessions as a steppingstone to trust-building. I'm not suggesting you give the house away or randomly offer up items in dispute. Be intentional. Plan a concession strategy in advance where possible so you can offer up a concession that will be of value to the other side but is an easy give for you.

Be sure to name your concessions as you do so. Don't just expect the other party to recognize the concession you've made or its value. As women, we can be particularly guilty of this. In our personal and professional lives, we sometimes sacrifice our needs and martyr ourselves in our quest to people-please. Yet, resentments build up when the corresponding appreciation doesn't seem to be forthcoming. We assume our efforts will be recognized and we'll be duly rewarded. Don't make this assumption. Identify your concessions and and note their value.

[See more on the art of concessions under Fundamentals of Negotiation]

Be Clear About Your Expectations and Explain Them

When identifying your 'needs' in a negotiation (which comes after listening to theirs as noted above), don't be vague or ambiguous or clever. Be clear. And be prepared to explain your needs. It's surprising how often we misperceive and attribute false motivations to the other party. You can avoid that problem by offering up your explanations in advance to assist in their understanding of your perspective. Communication builds trust.

Seek to Find Mutual Gains

Approach negotiations with a view to finding the highest good for all wherever possible. Don't just seek to have your needs met, but actively look for creative options to find mutually better solutions and outcomes.

Once we master trusting ourselves, trust involves a willingness to rely on someone else. There's a vulnerability inherent in the giving of it. Our past hurts often make this challenging. Exploring how to give trust allows us to live into being more trustworthy. It takes intentional practice . . . and it's worth it.

This simple ARE FIT model is the key foundation to up-levelling your negotiation prowess. Be intentional about making all six skills a regular part of your negotiation toolkit: Assertiveness, Rapport-building, Empathy, Flexibility, Intuition and Trust.

When women tell me they're nervous about the idea of negotiations, I remind them that they already use these skills every day in countless ways. It's just a matter of learning to be intentional in bringing them to the table in their negotiations. Step into the power and confidence that comes from knowing these traits are already feminine strong suits.

To help you in that process:

Go over the ARE FIT skills and list areas in your life where
you can now recognize that you already use these skills.
List as many as you can.
It doesn't have to be in negotiations.
Just think about where you already display assertiveness,
rapport-building, empathy, flexibility,
intuition and trustworthiness.
Don't be afraid to think outside the box.
Consider your personal and professional relationships.

When you're done, I invite you to brainstorm other areas in your life where you know you can apply these skills to get more of what you want, need and deserve.

By way of example, allow me to share a real estate experience we had where I invoked ARE FIT without even being conscious of it at the time.

We were looking at a large lakefront property for sale (which was well beyond our means at the time). I made it a point to learn as much about the current owner as possible. The owner had built the home himself and raised his family there but had health issues and was moving to a smaller, low-maintenance property now that his kids were grown with families of their own. My intuition told me to come back to the property for a second visit with our kids in tow and to meet in person with the homeowner in our interactions rather than indirectly through our respective real estate agents. I had our agent set up 'the meet'.

I commiserated with his situation and empathized with how difficult it must be to give up the home with its family memories. I shared the story of how my husband's parents had given up the family farm, but were lucky enough to pass it on to one of the sons. In this way, I built rapport and trust with the owner, with the added bonus that he could then picture this home he'd built with love carrying on as a home for another family. This turned out to be a key factor as unbeknownst to us at the time, it turned out that a Korean conglomerate was also bidding on the property, intending to tear down the house and build a small resort.

In addition to building rapport, I also demonstrated empathy, putting myself in his shoes, appreciating and mirroring his deep connection with this property (as opposed to our competition where it was a straight trans-actional real estate purchase). This built a kind of unspoken trust between us. When the conglomerate came in at a higher price-point than we were prepared to pay, who do you think the owner desired to deal with? At that stage we had to get assertive about our price point, but also be flexible to look at creative financing options, like a zero-interest vendor mortgage take-back. The savings in interest on the mortgage would bridge the wide gap in positions.

You can see how in this simple real estate deal, I invoked all six of the key skillsets to our benefit: assertiveness, rapport-building, empathy, flexi-bility, intuition, and trustworthiness. You too can bring ARE FIT to your negotiations, with intention to get better results, with higher satisfaction from the other party and improved relationships.

In the scenario above:

§ *Who do you think the vendor wanted to deal with?*

§ *Do you think my intuition to bring my family and meet face to face had any impact on the negotiation?*

§ *Do you think our empathizing with their situation played any role?*

§ *And what of the rapport-building? Who do you think the vendor was more interested in selling to—the family that they'd met, who wanted to carry on a new generation in the home they'd built or a conglomerate who wanted to tear it down?*

§ *Who do you think the vendors trusted more?*

I call these ARE FIT skills our 'secret weapons' as people have been conditioned to see feminine traits as weaknesses. I invite you to flip that perception. Turn that story upside-down. It's easier than you think to use these skills, which as noted above, you likely already use every day, to elevate your influence and persuasive abilities. In fact, as noted in the intro, people who invoke these qualities in their daily negotiations with intention, get better results, more creative solutions, better buy-in, better relationships, longer lasting deals and overall more positive impact.

The gift of this approach is that not only will it amplify your ability to get more of what you want personally, but it will create better solutions for everyone than could even have been contemplated under our current competitive model.

Imagine a world where we all negotiated from a place of powerful feminine persuasion. Where we sought to build stronger relationships. Not coming from a place of competition. Not seeking to just have our needs met. But instead, looking to understand and meet the needs of others, to value and respect our differences, to step into the best of our humanity. Imagine a world where we all chose to negotiate from that place. The ripple effect of that kind of transformation cannot be overstated.

III. Jade's Story

My first whisper of what I've come to call the Art of Feminine Negotia-tion™ came when my daughter, Jade, our firstborn, was diagnosed with a serious heart defect at only 2 months old and needed open heart surgery. She had an unusual little cough. Nothing dramatic. Our family doctor told me I was being paranoid when I'd asked about it. I was told she was fine at the one week, one month and two-month check-ups. Told she'd be the next President of the Baby Association (a clever play on my representation of trade union associations).

I'm not even sure what made me go for a second opinion. Call it femi-nine intuition. They say the universe is perfect and it certainly lined up for us that day. Turned out the pediatrician happened to be a cardiac specialist (unbeknownst to me at the time). He did the standard tests you'd expect. But the hair on the back of my neck rose when he took out a tiny blood pressure cuff (which I'd never seen before) and put it around her not-so-chubby leg and the furrow between his brow puckered even deeper.

"How old did you say she was?" he asked.

"Two months," I said.

"Well, if she's lived this long, I guess you'll be alright to go home for a few hours, but we need to get her to the hospital. I'll set it up and call you when it's arranged."

If she's lived this long? What the bloody …?!

And sure enough, by the time I got home he'd already called and left a message that I was to get to the emergency room at Sick Kids Hospital and ask for Dr. Dipshan, a cardiology fellow at the time. Dazed and more than a little confused, my husband and I headed downtown. Little did I know I wouldn't leave that hospital for almost three months.

Within minutes of arriving at the hospital, they had Jade hooked up to oxygen and whisked away. It was hard to find solid ground. Mere days before, I'd been told she was fine. *If she's lived this long* kept ringing in my head.

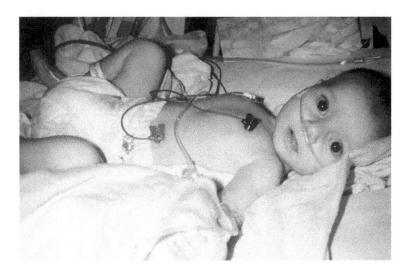

Of course, at this stage I was still in my masculine energy, so when two cardiologists sat us down to chat after an interminable barrage of tests, I said, "Don't sugar coat it. Give it to us straight."

And he did.

"Your daughter is in heart failure. She has a very serious heart defect and needs open heart surgery immediately or she won't live."

Have you ever had that feeling when, WHOOSH; your insides hollow out, and you're somehow hot and cold at the same time? I felt like saying, 'I've changed my mind. Maybe you can put a little sugar on that.'

Over the next few days, her diagnosis kept getting worse. We watched as the cardiologists argued over whether it was more dangerous to do a single surgery or split surgeries to deal with her multiple issues. Both sides felt equally strongly that she wouldn't survive the other's approach. That did not inspire confidence.

It didn't help that everything that could go wrong seemed to. If 99% of the population reacted one way to a drug or treatment, Jade always seemed to be the 1% that went the other way.

And you'd have thought if there was ever a time I'd bring my 'Barracuda' to the table that would have been it… when we were fighting for her life every day.

And yet, I didn't. I employed the A.R.E. F.I.T model before I had even developed the concept.

Every day in that hospital, operating solely on pure feminine strength and intuition, I was building rapport with the nurses, doctors and administrators—finding ways to build connection, to firmly place us all on the same 'team'.

I brought empathy to the table, commiserating with the nurses about being over-worked and undervalued, with the doctors about budget cuts and dealing with bureaucracy, with the administration about balancing service and budgets.

I had to stay flexible as the ground shifted beneath our feet from moment to moment with each new diagnosis, wrinkle or unexpected reaction.

I consistently tapped into my intuition (as medical terminology I'd never heard of before channeled through me as I advocated for my daughter).

And I had to build trust... with myself, and with all the players.

And was I assertive? You bet!

At first, we sat back and accepted their decisions. They were the experts after all. But when my tentative input at the beginning of the ordeal was routinely rejected only to turn out to be correct, and I'd been shushed a few times about questioning their approach only to find out my instincts were right, I started to trust my intuition. To use my voice, to go head-to-head with the country's leading cardiologists, setting my intuition alongside their medical degrees and decades of experience.

Like when Jade's fever spiked at ~ 4 months old and they tried to insist on a barrage of invasive tests for everything including meningitis, rejecting my suggestion that perhaps she was just teething as medically insupportable. And the next day her first tooth popped through tender gums and her fever dropped immediately.

Or when I wanted her off the ventilator as she'd been breathing through this artificial machine longer than she'd been breathing on her own, and every day she stayed on it reduced the chance she'd remember how to breathe again.

They said "No, she's not ready... she can't do it."

I had to dig for the strength to trust my intuition to insist they try. And I was grateful for the unconditional faith of my husband to trust my intuition against the advice of the experts. Especially as the seconds counted down after they grudgingly pulled the ventilator... and she wasn't breathing... and more seconds passed... and she still wasn't breathing.

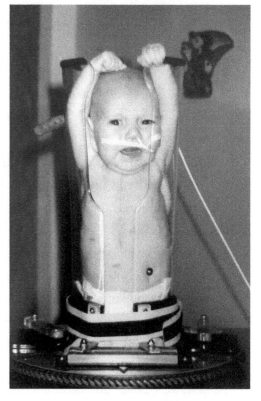

When they called "time's up" and clamored to reintubate, I found myself insisting (I don't know from where) "Just give her 5 more seconds!"

And time seemed to freeze as everyone in the room looked at each other, until one nurse just started counting.

"Five."

Come on, Jade.

I willed my thoughts to penetrate her silent space.

"Four."

You can do it, Jade.

"Three."

You're stronger than you think.

"Two."

Take my strength if you need it.

"One."

Like a scene from a soap opera, she finally sucked in that first breath on her own in months. Relief flooded my system and my knees turned to Jell-O.

But the relief was short-lived. They called us in as she approached 5 months old—barely back up to her birth weight—and told us we were at the end of the line. She wasn't responding and they believed they needed to go back in to operate again. It was the only option, they said.

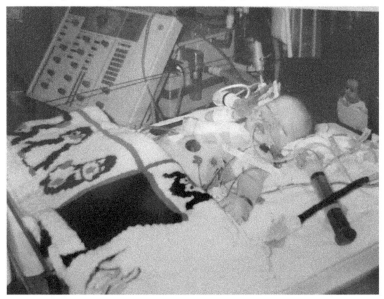

"No," I said. "She's not strong enough. She won't survive another surgery."

"Fine," said one of the cardiologists, shaking his head. "But we don't think she'll make it… and it will be on your head."

Wrong thing to say to the wrong woman at the wrong time. I didn't even have to speak before he knew he'd stepped into it.

Side note: sometimes body language and facial expressions can be more powerful than anything you might say.

They called for the Chief cardiologist to try to placate me.

"I understand you don't think we've done all we can. What is it you think we need to do, Mom?"

So I told him. In fact, I had a long list of simple, common sense items that I thought we needed to explore first.

"If we try these and they don't work will you let us operate?" he asked.

"If you try these and they don't work, I'll be begging you to operate," I said. "But I need to know we've exhausted all options given the high risk of another surgery in her fragile state."

And to their credit, they did it all.

And within a week, we were out of critical care and ready to go home.

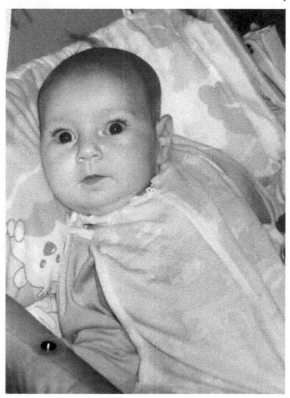

But I'd had to trust my intuition, bring the full force of my natural negotiation skills to the table every day.

I'm happy to report Jade is now 25 years old and against all odds and their predictions, she has never needed any further surgery or even heart medication again.

So why am I telling you this story?

Because the thing that saved Jade's life was negotiation. Every day for three months, hundreds of ongoing negotiations. And it wasn't until much later that I realized I hadn't brought that ball-busting, take-no-prisoners approach that I'd taken on in law. I was in Momma Bear mode, not a place of masculine energy. I was drawing on a skillset that is typically considered feminine… a skillset that you already have and use every day without thinking of it.

Imagine the power of tapping into that skillset with intention to get more of what you want and deserve in life?

I suspect, without me even being aware of it at the time, that was the genesis for the Art of Feminine Negotiation.

Feminine persuasion—HERsuasion™—is a powerful thing. It's why I feel compelled to share it with you. I want you to have everything you want and deserve… with ease.

FAST-TRACK INNER WORK TIPS

I hope your mind is opening to all the exciting possibilities of where and how you can start trying out these newly identified but familiar skills in more areas of your life. Now let's explore some practical tips to fast-track you to the next level of negotiation success.

I. Reframing Failure

You may be asking, if women have these superior skillsets that naturally position them to be effective negotiators, then why do so many women break out in a sweat at the idea of having to negotiate on their own behalf? What's holding them back from being the incredibly effective negotiators they could be? Why the resistance?

In addition to the obvious social conditioning we discussed earlier, we also touched on fear of failure as one key reason women are often held back in stepping into their power.

So allow me to try to shift your mindset on the issue of failure. I invite you to explore your concept of this dreaded word.

What if failure is the only path to sustainable success, if we need to fail our way to success? Most people assume that when they hit a failure (which we all will) it must mean you were headed down the wrong path and need to turn around and go in the other direction.

But what if, in fact, we have to go *through* failure to succeed? If failures are the stepping-stones on the road to our greatest success.

Thomas Edison 'failed' at creating the light bulb countless times before succeeding. In fact, it was only through those failures, and his persistence and willingness to fail that he achieved success. Is he known for the purported failures? No. He's lauded as a genius. Similarly, Abraham Lincoln purportedly failed twice in business, and lost 8 out of 10 elections before becoming President of the United States. Do people remember Lincoln for those failures? No. He's credited with abolishing slavery and considered by many to be the most influential U.S. President in history.

What if the women suffragists had given up fighting for the right to vote after being told 'no'? What if abolitionists like Harriet Tubman and the countless other brave women who fought against slavery had given up when told 'no'? You get the idea. It's through your failures that you learn, improve, grow and ultimately succeed. Maybe you just need to be willing to fail better.

I invite you to start a new tradition. Instead of mourning your failures and hanging your head in mortified dejection, I invite you instead to celebrate them. Incorporate failebrations[31], where you celebrate your failures and recognize their value—that without them you wouldn't find the way forward.

What's one thing you failed at today (or this week)?
What did you learn from it?
Enjoy a failebration this evening... celebrate your growth.

Imagine the power of incorporating this simple practice into your life. Every day, ask yourself what's one thing you spectacularly failed at that day. Then consider what you learned and celebrate. It will retrain your brain to embrace a growth mindset and quiet the inner critic that installs those limiting beliefs that hold you back.

II. Go For No

Getting Nos

In addition to our fear of failure, I'm going to go out on a limb and posit that women are also often held back by fear of rejection, of hearing the word 'no'. Studies confirm that women are less likely to ask for what they want than men. Where does that come from? What happened to our childhood ability to pester the heck out of our parents to get what we want? As kids, we seemed less afraid of the word 'no'. We got the message that if we persisted, we'd get what we want. But somewhere along the line that got conditioned out of us and we became afraid of rejection, of those 'nos'. It turns out that perhaps our instincts as kids were better on this front.

What if your fear of rejection, of hearing the word 'no' is the very thing standing between you and your best self? Between you and your kick-ass negotiator? Between you and getting what you deserve—from the boardroom to the bedroom? Perhaps what you need is a simple mindset shift.

In fact, some people believe that a negotiation never starts *until* you hear the word 'no', so resistance to negotiating past 'no' misses the point altogether. That theory is based on the idea that if you're asking for something you know you're going to get anyway and/or that the other side also wants, it's not really a negotiation at all.

If you accept that fear of hearing 'no' is a factor contributing to women's resistance to embracing negotiation, and we know that the best way to desensitize ourselves to the word is to get used to it, then how might we achieve that? How might you experience it so often that it loses its power over you? It's said that if you do the thing you fear, the fear will go away. If that's the case, it makes imminent sense that you take active steps to numb yourself to the word 'no'.

No doubt exposing yourself to receiving more 'nos' in your life requires you to get outside your comfort zone.

I was reminded of the limiting effects of comfort zones on a beach recently when I became entranced watching a hermit crab by my chair. It would pop up from its hole in the sand and skitter a few inches to the side, then stop. As soon as each wave started toward shore the hermit crab scurried back to cower in its bunker even though the waves never once came up to its hiding spot. I watched that poor little crab for ages and it never ventured more than a foot away from its hole. I could feel its desire. But I also felt its fear outweigh that desire over and over again.

It made me realize that we lull ourselves into believing our comfort zones are safe, when in reality they are self-imposed prisons. Those comfort zones will shrink and eventually suffocate us if we don't venture outside them and risk living. Do you want to live your life playing safe in a zone that never stretches your boundaries, that gets smaller and smaller so you can never be the biggest, best possible version of yourself?

Where are some areas in your life where you're staying stuck in a comfort zone?

What if, instead, you made a commitment today to step outside your comfort zone? Are you open to condition yourself by hearing 'no' as a way to the next level? What if, in thinking about rejection, and 'no', you opted to turn the paradigm on its head and instead of fearing it, you looked forward to it as a source of empowerment? How? The answer is so simple it's brilliant in its simplicity.

Ask. Ask. Ask. Pick practice areas in your life where you're willing to try asking for what you want. And here's the key. Don't be attached to getting a 'yes'. In fact, as proposed by Andrea Waltz and Richard Fenton in their bestselling book, *Go For No*,[32] instead of going for 'yes', actively go for 'no'. Embrace the possibility of multiple rejections and set your targets for how many 'no' answers you need to get the number of 'yes' answers you want.

By way of simple example, if you want 10 new clients this week (or donations to a cause or whatever you may be seeking) and you know you're likely to only get 10% of those you canvass to say 'yes', then don't set your sights on achieving 10 'yeses', but rather, flip that thought process on its head and set your goal to get 100 'nos'. That way, even as you get some 'yeses', you don't slow down. You keep going for the 'nos'. And when you hit the 'nos' (as you invariably will), it won't stop you—you won't see it as failure because you're going for them.

In addition to desensitizing yourself to the 'nos', think how much more likely you are to hit a higher level. Better yet, you'll lose all the angst and wasted negative energy that comes from being afraid of the rejection. Go for the no. It's liberating. You can show up as a more relaxed, authentic version of yourself. Such a simple concept and such a powerful tool to be able to release your fear of failure and step into the fabulous success that's waiting for you on the other side.

Are you willing to put yourself out there and go for that 'no'? To push past that fear of rejection. Push past that fear of getting a 'no', knowing that your success lies on the other side of it. Think of 'no' as the opportunity to problem solve to find your overlapping interests.

Here's a powerful question to assist in that problem-solving process. Every time you get a 'no', pause, smile and ask, *"I'm curious, what would it take to make this a 'yes'?"* That simple question opens the door to mean-ingful dialogue to move away from the 'no' and turn it into a 'yes'. It can uncover those pesky unstated needs to allow you the opportunity to redress them. At the very least, it's a valuable approach to fact-finding from which you can mine gems for moving forward.

Once you desensitize yourself to hearing 'no' and rid yourself of that fear, look out world… you'll be ready to level up, to step into your femi-nine power as the formidable negotiator you're ready to be.

If so, I invite you to:

Make a list of all the things you're going to ask for this week.
Pick at least 5 things per day that
you're going to ask for over the next 5 days.
Pick a target number of 'nos' that you're going to go for.
Start a preliminary list of some of the people you're going
to ask for each of those things.

You can make some small asks but be sure to also include some big bold asks. You may be surprised how liberating it is.

Giving Nos

In addition to learning to *accept* nos in your life, it's equally important to learn to *give* them. Our conditioning to be people-pleasers can make it challenging for many women to set boundaries. We try to do everything for everyone and in the process keep putting our own priorities, dreams, and vision on hold.

I invite you to take control of your time by eliminating, delegating, or automating those time-sucks that do not serve to move you closer to your goals. In my best-selling book, *How to Be a Woman On Purpose*, I take you through a simple exercise to kickstart the process.

Since you bought this book, you can access your free copy of this game-changing Time Audit at www.ArtOfFeminineNegotiationBook.com.

First, you'll want to change your mindset around giving nos. Remember that every time you say yes to something, you're saying no to something else. We all have the same 1440 minutes in a day. Prioritizing how you spend those minutes determines your ability to negotiate your best life.

Always allow yourself a pause before committing your valuable time. Tell the person asking that you'll get back to them. Give yourself time to consider if the request is something you want to do and if it's consistent with your values and/or moves you toward your own agenda. In addition to setting healthy boundaries and opening space for yourself, saying no to others often gives them (or someone else) the chance to step up for the opportunity and grow in the process.

Saying no doesn't have to be an unpleasant experience. You're not rejecting the person, just the requested task at hand. Saying something like – "Thanks for thinking of me for this! Sounds interesting! I'm currently working on 'x' so my schedule is maxed out at the moment. Maybe next time." – will soften the no and leave no hard feelings. You can even offer alternatives, suggesting other candidates who may be available.

Remember that the more you say no to things that don't move you toward your own vision, the more time you free up to engage in activities that do get you where you want to go.

III. Trust Your Natural Negotiation Style

I grew up in a rent-controlled tenement complex—a string of grey on grey block buildings, the only color the orange-rusted balconies. My dad worked shift work in a factory. I remember those early mornings or late nights, if I was up and able to catch him alone as he got ready to go to work. Watching those strong worker's hands pull the laces taut on his tan work boots or watching his man-stance as he squatted to see himself in the hall mirror, combing his hair back in that Elvis style pompadour (or whatever they were called). I loved those stolen moments. But I also remember the struggles. The fighting between my parents. There was never quite enough money to make ends meet.

My dad was a guy's guy. He was a big man, broad shouldered, big voice, big laugh, filled every room he ever walked in. Though he never taught my sister and I to box, I remember once when I asked, he had me assume the position and proceeded to sneak inside my Swiss cheese fist frame to tap me on the cheek over and over again, showing me how easy a target I was. I'm sure that wasn't his intention, but that's how it felt to me. Like an indictment. I wasn't a boy. I wasn't enough.

My paradigm shift came in grade 2. I won an 'academic' award. Maybe you remember them—those little badges they handed out for exceptional achievement. A light went on. Maybe I could achieve as a girl. And I became driven. I was going to have a different outlook for my family.

Initially I was gently pushed to pursue a traditional 'successful' career. Hence my single-minded path to a career in law despite my love of the arts.

And in law school (as I shared in the earlier 'Who Am I?' section of this book) I took a negotiations course where our entire grade was based on simulated negotiations. Definitely a competitive model with a highly competitive top law school student body. At the end of the year, the professor approached me and said he'd never seen results like mine in all his years of practice and teaching the course. I won virtually every single negotiation. And you can imagine those wins got harder as the school year went on and everybody was gunning for me, expecting this hard-ass negotiator, thinking they had to bring their A-game, expecting to be screwed over. Trust-building got harder and harder. But somehow, by just being myself, by being real, I was always able to win them over, to build that relationship, to find a win where they walked away happy.

I didn't approach those negotiations as zero-sum, winner-take-all interactions. I built rapport and trust; brought empathy, flexibility and intuition to the table; and ultimately relied on assertiveness to hold firm when I believed I'd hit my sweet spot.

It wasn't until I started the actual practice of law—initially in an all-male-partner firm, and later in my own firm, but still in a male-dominated environment—that I lost my intuitive feminine style. I still got great results. I got positive feedback and reinforcement for tearing people apart. I made people cry on the witness stand. At some point, I didn't recognize myself anymore. I felt disconnected. It didn't feel good. Or right.

And then it began to spill over into other areas of my life. I found I brought my 'tough' negotiator to every problem. Crappy hotel room? Look out, I was down at the front desk giving them what for. Phone company over-charging? Internet not working and the provider trying to blame the router provider? Hide your children, I was not letting them pull one over on me. And forget the 'get more with honey' approach. I'd convinced myself that people invariably tried to take advantage if you showed any sign of weakness; that the only way to get quick fulsome results was bringing my badass to the table. The little girl whose dad didn't teach her to box was Muhammad Ali in the ring of life.

Then one day I was having what I thought was a simple discussion with my son. I saw his frustration mounting and at some point, he finally exploded. "Mom! Does every conversation with you have to be an argument that you win?" And just like that, my world changed. I felt my heart rip as I saw the angst and hurt on his face. And my world view changed in an instant. My sense of self shattered into little pieces on the floor in front of me.

In that moment of profound connection, my perspective on effective negotiations flipped. I realized I'd bought into a myth about what it meant to be a skilled negotiator. I'd bought into the myth that it's a 'man's world' and that I had to adopt the masculine model for success. And I saw it for the myth it was. I realized that I didn't have to take that approach.

So started my journey to uncovering my ARE FIT method. In addition to tapping into and applying those 'feminine' ARE FIT skills to each negotiation, I also invite you to choose what negotiation style you adopt in any given negotiation. Again, both of these choices should be invoked with intention to improve the results you get.

What do I mean by negotiating style? There are different approaches that can be brought to bear in any negotiation. The way in which someone chooses to approach the interaction can determine the outcome, both positively and negatively. Most people automatically adopt their 'natural' negotiating style. In other words, they don't make a decision about how they want to show up. Instead, their default setting kicks in without them even being aware they had a setting at all.

There are some basic recognized styles of negotiation:

➤ Competing (I win, you lose)
➤ Avoiding (I lose, you lose)
➤ Collaborating (I win, you win)
➤ Accommodating (You win, I lose)
➤ Compromising (I win some, I lose some, You win some, You lose some)

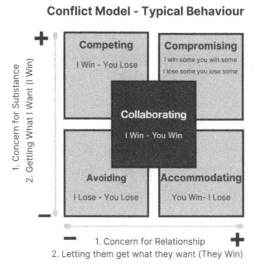

Conflict Model - Typical Behaviour

Which style one adopts typically depends, in part, on how much the person values relationship vis-a-vis substance. While not cast in stone, the following observations can often be made about each style:

Competing

➤ Likely to pursue their own agenda and interests, even at the expense of the other party.

➤ Higher in assertiveness and lower in cooperation.

➤ More focused on substance than relationship.

Avoiding

➤ Driven by a desire to avoid conflict or tension, not likely to pursue their own interests. While they don't necessarily pursue the other party's interest either, the avoidance can sometimes have that effect.

➤ Lower in both assertiveness and cooperation.

➤ Not necessarily focused on substance or relationship (although they often convince themselves—mistakenly—that they are protecting the relationship through their avoidance).

Collaborating

➤ Likely to seek solutions to fully satisfy all parties.
➤ High in both assertiveness and cooperation.
➤ Focused on and promoting both substance and relationship.

Accommodating

➤ Likely to put the needs of the other party ahead of their own.
➤ Lower in assertiveness and high in cooperation.
➤ Focus on relationship over substance.

Compromising

➤ Typically results in moderate satisfaction for both parties.
➤ Mid-range in assertiveness and cooperation.
➤ Focus on maintaining some relationship while securing some substance.

It's important to know your natural negotiating style. We all typically have a go-to style that comes more naturally to us. If you're uncertain, it's usually your default style when under pressure (i.e. how do you show up under stress?) Don't try to emulate someone else's style no matter how effective it may be for them. If it's not natural for you, it usually won't work.

Over the years in my law practice, I had many junior lawyers try to emulate my negotiation style. It didn't work. I would lead them to a discovery of their own natural negotiation style and encourage them to hone that style, to bring the broad range of negotiation skills to the table in their distinctive way. Trying to fit my style meant they weren't able to show up authentically. This interfered with their ability to build rapport and trust (both critical to securing best outcomes).

Having said that, circumstance can and should determine your style sometimes. Your natural default style may not be the best style for a particular negotiation. The key is flexibility. An effective negotiator can switch negotiation styles. Just be sure to make each style your own rather than trying to copycat someone else's version that doesn't fit you. If you decide you need to take a competing style on a particular issue, for example, that doesn't mean you need to beat your chest or pound the table because your counterpart's competition style looks like that. Find a way to bring the style you need to the table in a way that can still be authentic for you.

Think of it as choosing and wearing your style. You wouldn't be likely to borrow someone's dress or power suit going into an important meeting if it didn't fit. If it's too tight, you wouldn't want to be squeezing into it and if it's too loose, you wouldn't want it sagging off you. Either would look and feel awkward and negatively impact your confidence, your credibility and your presence (and accordingly undercut your persuasive abilities and influence). Wearing a negotiating style that doesn't fit works the same way.

What style you adopt will depend, in part, on the weight you give the following factors:

➤ Relationship with the other party
➤ Substantive/economic outcome
➤ Value of negotiation

Knowing your natural style, but also knowing the other styles, and considering which to bring with intention will up-level your negotiation prowess. And the flip side of that coin is also important. Raising your awareness and recognizing the negotiating style of the other party will similarly improve your outcomes.

Another element of knowing and trusting your natural negotiation style is showing up as your full authentic self. Do you feel comfortable being you, or do you rein in certain qualities to meet expectations (real or perceived)?

Women are more likely to modify their behaviour to meet expected social norms. We fear (with good reason) being judged as too emotional or too demanding. We may demure and soften our pitch and/or approach, ask for less, or play to egos in the room. At the other end of the spectrum, as discussed earlier, we may overcompensate, bringing masculine energy to the table that doesn't reflect our authentic style, believing that's the only way to be heard or succeed.

Many so-called experts advocate for women to modify their behaviour and employ workarounds to avoid push-back based on societal expectations. I do not subscribe to this theory. I think it perpetuates the stereotypes and entrenches the problem. If we want meaningful change, we need to start coaxing the elephant in the room out of the corner and into the light. I believe we're better served by showing up in our full authenticity, and in so doing, starting to break down ill-informed barriers and expectations. We get what we tolerate in life. If we continue to tolerate differential treatment and expectations, we will continue to attract them.

What's your natural negotiation style?
Consider a time when you went against
your natural style and think about what happened.
Did it work? Why or why not?
Then consider a time when you invoked
your natural negotiation style.
How did that feel compared to going against
your natural style?
Did it work? Why or why not?

IV. Invoke Your Momma Bear

As discussed earlier, assertiveness is one of the skills required of an effective negotiator. Also as discussed, women tend to rank lower—or at least believe they rank lower—in this area even though they can be fierce advocates on behalf of someone else. When a woman advocates for her child, for example, she brings it! Some people refer to this as the lioness syndrome, but I like to refer to it as invoking the Momma Bear.

If I suggested you get between a Momma bear and her cub, what would your knee-jerk reaction be? No doubt your brain would scream 'No!' with a corresponding emotional reaction somewhere between angst and abject terror. Why? Because everyone knows that Momma bears are commanding when protecting their young. And I bet if I asked you to think of a time when the Momma bear in you reared her head, you could come up a number of examples. But I also bet that in virtually every one of those examples you were defending someone else, whether a child, loved one, or other perceived vulnerable underdog.

So, it's obvious that women have the capability to stand in a place of assertiveness. We've just been reluctant to use that particular modality for our own needs. We tend to hold back when self-advocating. As we've noted before, this isn't surprising given our social conditioning. That same self-effacing fear of being shunned that kicks in as early as kindergarten, carries on through life as women anticipate that being assertive in self-advocacy situations will evoke judgment, pejorative attributions (i.e., she's a 'b*t#h') and backlash (i.e., exclusion). And so, we rein in our assertiveness, shy away from competing tactics and accordingly may obtain lower outcomes. Yet when we advocate for someone else, we don't expect backlash so don't hedge and get better results.

This shows us that women aren't less *capable* as bargainers. We aren't less *able* to bring assertiveness to the table. Rather, we can adjust bargaining styles depending on the perceived needs of a situation. We do have this skill. We can choose. We just need to tap into it regularly when negotiating for ourselves.

So why is it that you can bring your badass self to advocate on behalf of others, but you leave her locked in a closet at home when you need to champion yourself? What if you turned that paradigm on its head and decided to invoke your Momma bear for the bear cub in you?

Yes, you have a little bear cub inside you. We all do. Think of all your 'little girl' insecurities, fears, feelings of 'not-enoughness' or inadequacy. All those unhealed hurts you still carry. Why not invoke your Momma Bear for that bear cub in you? It's so uncomplicated. A simple, subtle mind shift that allows you to step into your assertive self and in so doing improve your negotiation success.

Now you might be asking, "Hey, Cindy. I thought you said negotiation isn't all about the bark and bite—that the tough guy doesn't always win? And I thought you said women possess the skillset to be formidable negotiators in spades and that assertiveness isn't the only determinative skill in who wins negotiations?" All true. But if you've read carefully, I've also said that women have been duped into believing that they aren't very accomplished in assertiveness and this makes them less likely to *think* they can change and/or exercise control over their circumstances. As a result, women often go into negotiations already doubting they can change their circumstance. This is dangerously disempowering for a negotiator.

So, while women already shine in most of the skillset categories, I'd like to see us step into our feminine power potential in the 'assertiveness' category as well. I invite you to challenge old beliefs and start tapping into your natural skillset. This is just an extension of that. I'm calling on you to challenge any resistance or belief you may hold that you can't (or shouldn't) exercise assertiveness. I'm hoping to break an old pattern so you can avoid breaking out in a sweat at the idea of negotiating on your own behalf for something you want. Let's make some new patterns instead.

What if the key to your power to take your negotiations to the next level lies in your ability to better love yourself? Next time you have to bargain for something for yourself, tap into the inner bear cub in you—that potentially frightened, vulnerable, needy cub. Call on your Momma Bear to love and protect her. Step outside yourself for a moment and see your own deserving cub standing in your place, needing your help, needing your strength, needing its Momma bear to stand for it. Then be that Momma bear. Advocate for your own baby cub—the cub in you—as you would for anyone else you loved.

How simple and beautiful is that?

Can you think of a time when you invoked
your Momma Bear on behalf of someone else?
Consider how that worked and why.
Explore how you felt.
Then I invite you to think of your triggers–the ones that
bring out the little girl in you and make you shrink a bit.
Explore how you could invoke your Momma Bear for that
bear cub in you when you next face those triggers.

V. Control Your Focus

Your energy will flow where your focus goes. Your point of attraction will become your reality. And so, the direction of your focus is the direction of your life. Based on simple principles of the law of attraction, you will attract more of what you focus on… even if it's what you think you are trying to repel. In other words, if you focus on what's wrong, you will continue to see more of it in your life. And the opposite is also true. The more you focus on what's right, the more you will attract further positivity in your life.

Your brain gives you what it thinks you want. It determines what it thinks you want by the thoughts you feed it. If you expect the worst, your brain will look for examples to support the negative thoughts as it thinks it is giving you what you want. And so the self-fulfilling prophesy circle begins. Why not train your brain to give you the best, to think the best, to expect the best, and to look for examples of the best the world has to offer? Think what a shift to positivity that would open for you.

Monitoring your internal mental dialogue is an important part of that process. Consider the negative chatter that swirls around your existence. Perhaps, much of that negative chatter is in your head right now. I invite you to ask yourself:

'Does it serve me right now to allow this to take up space in my mind?'

Remind yourself that you DO control that. You control your thoughts and the meaning you give those thoughts. In fact, the meaning you attach to the thoughts you allow in determines your reality.

There are 3 decisions we make every moment. We need to be aware of them and control them:

1. What am I going to focus on?
2. What does it mean?
3. What am I going to do?

Never underestimate the power of your beliefs. When I started my own law firm, the power of my beliefs carried me through. Perhaps it was naiveté and the bliss of ignorance, but I never doubted that I would be successful in opening my own practice. In hindsight that baffles me. I had no money to speak of. No credit. No clients confirmed. I had no real business plan. But it never crossed my mind that I wouldn't achieve my goal. I just assumed that I could and would. It was an unshakable belief because it hadn't even crossed my mind to question it.

As a result, I showed up with unshakable confidence. And as a result of that, against all odds, I secured a line of credit and the clients started to come... in droves. Within a very short span I was hiring staff and leasing fancy digs in a spacious office downtown.

Had my inner critic been engaged, had I questioned the feasibility of my plan (or lack thereof), I likely never would have had the confidence to try. Or, I would have exuded such uncertainty that I couldn't have inspired the confidence that led to my successful outcome.

Be intentional about the words you use, including your silent internal mental chatter. According to the Cleveland Clinic, the average person has up to 60,000 thoughts/day.[33] Of those thoughts, 95% repeat each day. Sadly, on average, 80% of those repeated thoughts are negative.[34] Think of the destructive power of that negative repetition.

How does this impact on your negotiation abilities? As mentioned earlier, your first and most important negotiation is the one with yourself... negotiating your mindset. Choosing your focus is a critical component of that process. Part of the inner work we referenced in the introduction includes getting intentional about your thoughts and the meaning you attach to those thoughts.

If you show up to a negotiation believing you're unlikely to achieve your outcome, or feeling outgunned, or worried that you're 'less than', you are already self-sabotaging your chances of success. By contrast, if you expect the best possible outcomes, visualize your celebration, breathe in your certainty, you'll show up with the requisite confidence to move the dial in your favor.

Your thoughts are the gateway between where you are and where you want to go.

Change your words.

Change your thoughts.

Change your results.

VI. Negotiate Your Personal Apology Fast

How often do you apologize in a typical day? Do you find yourself saying 'sorry' when you accidentally bump into someone... or even when they bump into you? If you're guilty as charged, then I invite you to negotiate with yourself to go on an apology fast. Apologizing typically doesn't serve you. In fact, it can become a disempowering habit that undermines your credibility, confidence and self-esteem.

In any negotiation, it's important that you know and establish your value—both for yourself and for the other party. Chronic apologizing undercuts your value. It undermines your own confidence and sends a message to the other party that you (and accordingly your needs) don't matter as much.

I recently accepted a challenge for an apology fast when Social Confidence Coach & Expert, Dr. Aziz[35], pointed out to me how often I said "Sorry" over the course of our 4-day Mastermind event together. As a Canadian woman I'm doubly challenged in that regard.

Women tend to apologize more than men. That's perhaps not surprising after a lifetime of conditioning to be people-pleasers. It's also not surprising when you consider that as women, we tend to live our lives based on other people's expectations of us, looking for external validation rather than finding it internally.

As children, we're taught that apologizing is polite and expected.[36] Yet interestingly, parents tend to expect apologies more from daughters than sons[37]—as if young girls inherently have more to apologize for. Or at least, I wonder if that's what we take away from it. That somehow, we ought to feel the need to beg forgiveness for wanting things, the need to justify our desires and decisions.

This shame response arises in part from a need to belong and for acceptance. What if you turned that habit on its head? What if you decided that you were entitled to want things without guilt or fear of judgment? That you're entitled to have a voice, be heard, and take up space without asking to be excused for it? What if you didn't need to justify yourself, didn't need others' approval or permission? What if, today, you decided that you're entitled to negotiate your life on your terms?

I invite you to consider how often and in what circumstances you currently apologize. As mentioned above, do you apologize when you accidently bump into someone, or even when they bump into you? How about when you sneeze? Maybe even when someone interrupts *you*? Do you preface unwelcome news with 'I'm sorry to say'? Or leave a 'Sorry I'm not here' or 'Sorry I missed your call' message on your voicemail? Do you even apologize to your pets? We often apologize reflexively.

Do you sometimes say sorry for things you're not sorry about but expect may have displeased the other person? Maybe you went out for the night and that meant your partner (or boss or whoever was affected) had to step up to take care of something you normally would have done. When they mention it do you reflexively apologize even though you enjoyed your night out and know you deserved it?

Women often do this in our self-appointed role as peacekeepers, to try to restore balance in the relationship. At the other end of the spectrum, do you ever find yourself apologizing when you're really asserting your needs, desires or rights? For example, instead of saying "Please turn down that #@!* T.V.," you say, "I'm sorry, I can't concentrate with the T.V up so loud." Or instead of saying "I'm not going to pay for that package because I didn't order it," you say, "I'm sorry, I didn't ask for the upgraded package."

Do you worry that not softening these positions with a "sorry" will seem aggressive, thoughtless, offensive, or less feminine? Perhaps these patterns are left-over vestiges from generations of having to maneuver to have our needs met in perceived socially palatable or acceptable ways in a society where we had so few rights. Maybe it's time to recognize that pre-emptive apologizing no longer serves you and acknowledge it's time to let it go.

Some negotiation experts advocate using the apology as a negotiation strategy to get what you want—to soften the 'ask'. I caution this approach for women, who already tend to over-apologize. While it's admittedly important to apologize when you cause real injury to another (whether emotional or physical), I invite you to choose your apologies with care and intention. There are significant downsides to excessive apologizing.

➤ Psychologists suggest that compulsive apologizing presents as weakness, reflecting lack of confidence and sending the message that you're ineffectual.[38] Some go so far as to posit that it gives permission to others to treat you poorly. [39]

➤ At the other end, studies suggest that refusing to express remorse increased self-esteem, sense of control and empowerment.[40]

➤ Added to that, consider that you may be doing a disservice to the people you're apologizing to. Neuro-scientists found that both giving and receiving apologies pumped up cortisol levels in our brains as they triggered 'survival emotions' like anger, disgust, shame, fear, etc.[41]

➤ Apologizing can open unnecessary doubt, introducing the idea you've done something wrong and causing others to attribute blame they otherwise wouldn't have contemplated.

➤ It can also trigger internal guilt and self-blame, which undermines confidence, and ironically induces more apologies in a toxic destructive cycle.

➤ Habitual apologizing also dilutes your apologies. If you're constantly apologizing over things that don't warrant it, your sincere apologies will have less impact and won't land. You run the risk that all your apologies come across as disingenuous and meaningless.

➤ Chronic apologizers often annoy and irritate others and tend to cause people to tune them out.

None of these impacts serve your needs, personally or professionally.

How do you train yourself out of apologizing? The first step is to increase your awareness. To that end, I challenge you to track your apologies over the next week. Get an accountability partner or partners if need be. Once you have a handle on how often and in what circumstances you apologize, find easy ways to change your language or flip the script.

Here are some examples of simple reframes you can try on for size:

➤ If you make an error and it gets pointed out, rather than saying "I'm sorry", try "thanks for catching that".

➤ If someone is trying to push past you, rather than a reflexive "Sorry", try "Here, let me get out of your way".

➤ Don't feel the need to apologize for saying 'no'. If you want to decline an invitation, practice resisting the urge to say "Sorry" and instead simply say "I can't make it. Maybe next time."

➤ If you bump into someone by accident, instead of 'Sorry', say 'excuse me', 'pardon me', 'go ahead', or 'after you'.

➤ If you're running late, instead of apologizing, try 'thanks for waiting for me'.

You get the idea. This is just a teaser to get you thinking of alternative ways of expressing yourself. These may seem like irrelevant semantics, but our language matters. The more you raise your awareness about the language choices you make, and the more you get intentional about weeding out language which undercuts your power, the more you'll increase your influence and persuasive abilities.

I'm officially throwing down the glove and challenging you to go on an apology fast. Negotiate with yourself to stop saying 'sorry'. Instead, re-train yourself to find more empowering ways to communicate that allow you to stand in your power and not dilute your confidence, credibility or self-esteem.

This is not to say that you should never apologize. Of course, when you have caused harm or when you find you're in the wrong, it is not good strategy to go silent, or ignore the other party or focus on trying to spin it, or continue to defend a position you no longer believe in.

Many people assume that acknowledging an error or acknowledging you don't know something will adversely impact on your credibility. In fact, the opposite is usually true. Owning up to errors and/or admitting you don't know (and undertaking to find out information) builds trust in relationships and increases your credibility.

If you find you're on the wrong side of an argument, acknowledge that fact. Give credit to the other party for raising your awareness on that particular issue. Be prepared to offer a simple and sincere apology. And that's it. Don't try to defend your past position. Don't draw out the acknowledgement or apology, making it awkward and a bigger deal than it needs to be. This simple strategy will serve to build better relationships and with it, better outcomes.

And don't beat yourself up. You made a mistake. So what? We all do. So long as you learn from the mistake, leave the guilt in the past where it belongs.

VII. You Get What You Tolerate

You get what you tolerate. What do I mean by that? Am I saying that everyone is responsible for everything that happens to them in life? No. History is replete with examples of people in absolutely untenable situations not of their own doing. Having said that, as a basic life lesson or starting point, you could do worse than embracing and operating from the philosophy: you will get what you tolerate. This holds true in life. It also holds true in negotiations.

Let's start, as always, with your first negotiation: with yourself. What you tolerate of and for yourself is what you'll get. As noted earlier, we often stay in our comfort zone, afraid of the unknown; afraid of pushing our limits; afraid to challenge status quo, our own beliefs, the beliefs of those in our life. This is a mistake. Staying in the comfort zone inevitably leads to stagnation in one form or another. You won't reach your full potential by staying comfortable. You won't achieve your dreams or fulfill your vision by hanging back in your comfortable space. Few people reach the end of their life and feel relieved at having played it safe. Most end-of-life regrets are for chances not taken, experiences not lived.

The good news is that it's not too late. It only takes a simple mindset shift. More good news? You control your own thoughts. Simply make a decision that you won't tolerate mediocrity from yourself anymore. Demand more of yourself. Decide what you want in life and make a pact with yourself that you won't tolerate anything less. Choose to push yourself outside your comfort zone. I'm not suggesting you need to turn your world upside-down overnight. But start. Take one step outside your comfort zone, towards a larger vision for yourself. And then another. Every journey, big and small, starts with a decision to take a step in that direction.

As you tackle your internal negotiation about what you'll tolerate of yourself, also start the internal dialogue about what you're prepared to tolerate of other people. If you want different results, you need to take different action. You set the tone for how you will be treated. Take ownership of that. If you find yourself thinking, I *wish so-and-so wouldn't keep doing that!* maybe it's time you turn the lens on yourself. Why have you been tolerating it? What can you do to stop tolerating it?

As women, we often aspire to be (or at least appear) easy-going. We tend to people-please. Added to that, we suffer from the debilitating belief that it's selfish to put our needs first. And so, we put the needs of our partners, kids, co-workers, parents—the list goes on—ahead of our own needs. And guess what happens? Those people come to expect that you will continue to put their needs first. Maybe at first they're really appreciative (or not) but invariably at some point it gets taken for granted. Why? Because you tolerated it. And what you tolerate is what you get.

I'm encouraging you to choose to recognize—NOW—that tolerating this pattern does not serve you. It stands in the way of you realizing your own dreams, aspirations, goals, vision, and desires. It stands in the way of you becoming the best version of yourself.

At some point, this tolerance typically leads to built-up tensions, resentments, anxiety, negativity—all mixed with a healthy dollop of guilt (because we women are so good at doing guilt).

Also consider that not only does it not serve you, it doesn't serve those around you. When you consistently subjugate your own needs to those of others, think of the role model you're setting for your daughters or other young women—that their needs as women, mothers, etc. are less important. Think of the message you're sending your sons or other young men—that their needs will be more important than any women in their life as they grow into men.

You're also training those in your life to devalue you. That it's okay to take advantage of you. In so doing, you not only sell yourself short, you turn them into a lesser version of themselves.

For what it's worth, I'm not preaching from on high here. I come to you with these nuggets of wisdom having learned on the hard road of experience. I spent many decades training people that I cared about in my life to take advantage of me. It caused me much heartache. It cost me many relationships. And it also cost those I thought I was being generous to. They became smaller, uglier versions of themselves, unable to achieve their full potential.

So in addition to the tired old analogy about putting on your own oxygen mask first in a Mayday plane situation, next time, instead of playing that same old track in your mind that you're selfish if you don't keep giving more than you get, maybe you choose to recognize that it's actually more selfish to deprive them of the opportunity to be their best self.

How do you change those patterns?

After you choose to stop tolerating patterns that don't serve you, start being clear about your expectations. Don't assume or expect that people would (or should) know what you want or need, or what's fair, reasonable or appropriate.

Don't let what you get depend on what others may decide. You need to be clear about what *you* want and to communicate those expectations unequivocally.

If someone doesn't meet your expectations, don't stew or simmer or let it go 'this time'. Discuss the issue right away and reinforce your expectations. Make sure you've determined what the consequences will be when someone doesn't meet your expectations… and stick to it! Otherwise, you're on the slippery tolerance slope that, much like an icy ski hill, ends with someone getting hurt.

At the outset, I said that history is full of examples of people who ended up in situations they didn't deserve and that were not of their making. But it should be a strong lesson to us that even in many extreme examples through history, the vast majority of tyrannies and atrocities didn't happen overnight. There was typically a long lead up. Many warnings. People tolerated ever-increasing injustices, cruelties and intolerable behavior and in so doing, the tolerances became higher, the bar became lower and the way was paved for unthinkable end results.

Don't allow this to happen in your life—personally or professionally. Be vigilant to your own tolerances. Speak up when behavior doesn't match your expectations.

You get what you tolerate. So monitor your tolerance and don't wait until a fatal tipping point is reached.

I invite you to consider 3 things in your life that you've been tolerating that perhaps you ought not.
Then, brainstorm how you're going to change that pattern.
Come up with some concrete steps and ideas of how you're going to stop tolerating them.

VIII. A Rising Tide Lifts All Boats

Given long-time limitations imposed on women, it's not surprising that many women operate from a scarcity mindset. With limited job opportunities available beyond the proverbial glass ceiling, it seemed like a competition of many for few. Women deprived themselves of the value in supporting each other on the path to success.

Today, with the rise of the feminine, we're finally seeing a corresponding recognition that a rising tide lifts all boats. Women are more intentional about inspiring, uplifting, and elevating other women. In so doing, we elevate ourselves. Abundance mindsets, seeking to expand the pie (rather than grab a share of a fixed pie), open unexpected opportunities and benefit all.

Coming from a place of grace, generosity, and service has profound positive benefits for the giver. As noted by Alex Hermozi, author of *$100M Offers*, "People who help others (with zero expectation) experience higher levels of fulfillment, live longer, and make more money." With that philosophy in mind, he posed this simple question to his readers:

Would you help someone you've never met, if it didn't cost you money, but you never got credit for it?

I'd like to echo that question for you to consider.

I'm on a mission to help women leverage their natural power to get more of what they want and deserve in life through the Art of Feminine Negotiation™. To achieve that goal, I need to reach them. To reach them, they need to discover this book. One sure-fire way to increase the likelihood of them finding it is through reviews. So, here's my ask. If you think this book would benefit other women, please take a moment now to leave a review. It costs nothing but a moment of your time.

That review might help another woman …

➤ Find her voice
➤ Get the recognition she deserves

➤ Make more money
➤ Improve her relationships
➤ Rediscover her life as she sets boundaries and prioritizes her dreams

Think of the power your simple review wields. A moment of your time could change a life. Share the gift of empowerment. Thanks for considering this!

HOW TO USE THE 5 WS TO UP-LEVEL YOUR BARGAINING

We're taught to implement the 5 Ws in problem solving or information gathering. To be clear, I'm not talking about the multi-purpose lubricant touted for everything from squeaky doors to rusty under-carriages. I'm talking about those 5 little words—who, what, where, when and why. Not only are those simple five monosyllabic words helpful in investigatory endeavors, but they can have profound impact in other areas of life. Negotiation is no exception. In fact, I'd go so far as to say those negotiators who consider the 5 Ws, with intention, set themselves apart and can better navigate the sometimes-murky waters of mediation and negotiation.

I invite you to incorporate the 5W model as a fundamental part of your negotiation preparation. Go through the 5W checklist, with intention, as you get ready for any negotiation or difficult conversation.

I. Know the Who

Who are you?

This may seem like a ridiculous question but trust me when I say it's definitely worth giving this query serious consideration. Knowing yourself is a key first step to any effective negotiation. Knowing your strengths, weaknesses and triggers are important items to factor in to your strategy and tactics.

Learning Styles

Tied to this, we all have different learning styles. Some tend to be more auditory learners, while others are visual and still others are kinesthetic. This will make a difference in how you receive information. Do you know your preferred learning style? Consider how you best absorb information and ensure you get what you need in the way you need it.

It should also factor in to how you *give* information in your negotiations. To do this effectively, ideally you want to know the natural learning style for the other party you are negotiating with. A good strategy is often to incorporate elements of all three learning styles into any presentation or pitch you make in your negotiations. This will increase the likelihood of your message landing and not getting lost by reason of mixed or cross learning styles.

How do you determine the learning style of the other party? If you have a longer standing relationship and you pay attention, it will usually be easy to determine someone's default learning style. If not, pay attention to their language.

While not cast in stone, auditory learners tend to use language like: "I *hear* you. I want you to *listen*. That *sounds* good. What do you *hear* that's holding you back?" Auditories are likely to complain that others are not *listening* to them.

By contrast, visual learners would be more likely to use language like: "Can you *see* what I'm saying? How do you *see* the situation? I can *see* that. This *looks* good." Visuals are most likely to complain about others not *seeing* things their way, or not making eye contact.

Not to leave out the kinesthetics in the crowd, a kinesthetic learner would be more likely to say, "Are you in *touch* with what I'm saying? How do you *feel* about this situation? I'm getting a *handle* on this. Let's *move* forward together on this." Kinesthetics may complain about others being insensitive.

How do you apply this? If you know you are a visual learner and you're finding it hard to follow the 'speech' across the table, then ask to see the proposal in writing. (Adopt as necessary depending on your preferred learning style). Why struggle through and risk missing something important that could work to your detriment rather than simply ensuring that you get what you need in the form in which you need it?

Likewise, if the other party is an auditory learner, don't just drop a fifty-page brief of proposals on their lap (unless your intention is to avoid clarity for them) but instead, make sure to explain the matter orally. If you're dealing with a mixed auditory and visual team on the other side (or even in the preparation for your own team) perhaps you prepare a video which has both visual and audio elements and/or speak to it and also provide a written proposal. For the kinesthetic learners in the crowd, maybe you visit a site in question for hands-on interaction or have a model available or give them an exercise to work out on the issue at hand.

This consideration applies in your personal life as well. Consider the learning style of your partner, kids, etc. and ensure you tap into their style to increase their receptivity for important conversations. It doesn't help to deliver what you believe to be a brilliant oratory on the perils of drug use to your 14-year-old visual-learning teen if their eyes are glassing over and they're not absorbing a word. Instead, maybe share a compelling video from a peer and go over some charts and visually interesting data. Start the conversation from that vantage point and you'll increase your odds of connecting.

Your goal is to be seen, heard, felt and, equally if not more importantly, to have the other party experience that they were fully seen, heard and felt. We listen with our hearts as well as our ears. Ultimately, you want your audience to feel, "Ah, she gets me. She understands me." That will build trust and with it the ability to get better outcomes. To do that you need to express your message to the eyes that see you, the ears that hear you, the heart that feels you. Much like we need to ensure we use the correct operating systems for our technology, we need to target our messaging to the correct 'operating system' of our bargaining counterparts. To do this effectively, you need to explore who you are dealing with and who you need to show up as to best connect.

Your Role and Perceived Authority or Position

If your negotiation is professional, what's your position, title, and authority? Is there a hierarchy at play, and if so, where do you fit in that hierarchy? Who will the other party see you as? Will they see you as someone to take seriously or someone they'll try to fluff off? Think about this and be prepared. Factor it into your strategy. Find a way to use this insight to your benefit. If the buck stops with you, use that. If not, find a way to make it advance your needs. If someone is likely to underestimate you, use that. Turn it to your advantage.

If this is a personal negotiation, are you coming into this negotiation as a mom, daughter, sister, wife or neutral? I had an experience recently where I was dealing with my daughter and I desired a particular outcome. As a mom, I was very invested in pushing for the outcome I wanted for her best interest. The conversation did not go well. I realized (too late) that if I were coaching a client on this issue, I would never have approached it the way I had. My passion in mom-mode sabotaged my effectiveness as a negotiator in my exchange. Had I been able to maintain a more neutral and compassionate approach I would likely have gotten infinitely better results—for her and me.

Similarly, with a life partner, we're much more likely to let emotion enter our bargaining and potentially undermine our position in ways we'd never contemplate or tolerate in a third-party situation. In advance of your discussion, consider, with intention, what role you want to negotiate from to maximize your effectiveness. Even though you're negotiating with your kid or life partner, you may or may not want to come at the negotiation in that 'role'. Be deliberate in making this decision. If your life partner is excited about an opportunity to start a risky new business venture, perhaps the conversation will go better if you approach it in compassionate-friend mode at the outset versus potentially-financially-adversely-impacted wife.

Who do you want to show up as?

You may be scratching your head, wondering what I mean by that. Relax, I'm not suggesting dress-up or role play. Every interaction, every moment of every day, you get to choose how you want to show up—*who* you want to show up as. Will you show up with compassion? Integrity? Presence? Generosity? Vulnerability? Or is this an exchange where you need to show up tough? Confident? Controlled? Calm? Compelling? You get the idea.

Making this decision consciously, in both your personal and professional life, can profoundly change your relationships and your interactions. Imagine choosing who you want to show up as every evening before you step through your front door or every morning before you step across the threshold at work. Imagine the power of choosing who you show up as for every exchange.

I invite you, as part of your preparation, to choose 3 words to describe who you want to show up as in any given negotiation. Don't stress about it. There's no right or wrong answer. It's your choice who you determine will best serve you. Be intentional about it. Have fun with it. Choosing your 3 words will allow you to stay grounded if you get triggered in the negotiation. Simply pause, breathe, recall who you decided to be… then find her again and carry on from that place.

Who will the other party expect you to show up as?

When deciding who you plan to show up as in your negotiation, also consider who the other side will *expect* you to show up as. This can be a powerful dynamic shift. When we show up differently than expected by the other party, it can change the balance and give you a distinct advantage as they attempt to adjust their perspective.

Again, this works both personally and professionally. As a parent, if your child expects you to show up as 'angry mom', but instead you show up with compassion and understanding, it will cut through the defenses and open unexpected space for more effective communication. Likewise, in a business setting, if the other party expects you to show up as an accommodating people pleaser, but instead you show up in a place of powerful assertiveness, it will shift the balance. And alternatively, if they expect you to show up as the 'Barracuda' and instead you show up with absolute empathy, it opens doors to new opportunities.

Who are you negotiating with?

Once you've examined yourself and decided who you're going to show up as in any given communication, do the same for the other party. Who are they likely to show up as? Consider this in advance of the meeting or discussion. For example, do you anticipate that they'll bring their game face with bluster and bravado and aggression, or play the victim card? Be prepared either way. Also consider if they show up differently, how could you best handle it? That way you can prepare in advance for most eventualities.

Who should you be negotiating with?

Have you ever conducted a negotiation with someone only to have them claim not to have authority to give you what you need at the end of the conversation? Perhaps before you decide how to handle your bargaining counterpart's approach, consider if they're even the best person to address the particular issue. If not, who should you negotiate with? Maybe it makes sense to have a preliminary discussion with the intended negotiator, but maybe you should resolve this issue right out of the gate and insist on speaking to the appropriate person from the outset for maximum efficiency and results.

Tied to that, consider who else can or should be included in the negotiations. Whether on your team or the other party's, who could help give you an edge? Maybe someone on your team has a particular viewpoint or expertise or style that would resonate deeply with your counterpart. If so, consider bringing them in. Likewise, maybe someone on the other party's team would be highly sympathetic to your proposal. If so, try to find a way to have them included.

The opposite is also true. Who should be excluded from the discussions if possible? If someone has an ax to grind with you, it might be prudent to find a way to keep them away from the table. If someone has a history of taking a hard line on the issue you need, try to bypass them. Or maybe, just having too many cooks stirring the broth is a problem in itself and culling the herd will yield you better results. Again, considering these angles with intention will elevate your bargaining and increase your effectiveness to get you better results.

On a few occasions in my law practice, we made calculated decisions to refuse to come to the table to negotiate on important issues while a particular manager remained at the table. These managers on each occasion had been caught lying, misrepresenting information, taking advantage of our members and/or treating our membership and its leadership with a complete lack of dignity or respect. Our refusal to come to the table on issues that the Employer needed to deal with, forced them to redress the bad apples on their teams. This dramatically increased the union's leverage going forward as it sent the message to other (and future) managers that they needed to play ball with the union or likely suffer potentially serious adverse personal consequences.

Again, this consideration of *who* you should negotiate with applies to both your personal and professional negotiations. In our house, there are certain conversations with our boys that I know will escalate unnecessarily if my husband takes part. And the opposite is also true. There are some issues where his particular approach will yield much better results than I'd be likely to secure.

Who will be impacted by your negotiation?

We sometimes forget about the ripple effect of our actions. Think about the potential impact of your bargaining on others who may not be at the table. Sometimes a shortsighted gain in the moment may have disastrous long-term impact on others. Negotiating a 'win' on one issue may negatively impact on other important relationships in your life. These are factors that a skilled negotiator will contemplate and incorporate in the preparation process. So should you if you want to up your game and get the best outcomes.

This factor would often raise its ugly head in my work as an attorney defending trade unions. A hot-button issue would arise and my client and its membership would be fired up to do battle. A more in depth consideration of the possible ripple effects of the argument on the table, however, would reveal that arguing for the 'win' on that discreet issue for a small group of affected members would require an interpretation of a particular clause (or sometimes even word) that would have disastrous consequences for the union when applied to other clauses of significantly more import for the entire bargaining unit.

This is intended to raise a smattering sample of *who* questions for you to contemplate. It's designed to open your perspective and show the benefits of a broader vision in bargaining.

If you do so with forethought and intention, you can move the dial to stack the odds in your favor. Take advantage of every possible edge. You'll have more influence, be more persuasive and get better outcomes in your negotiations. It's simple and powerful—like most great ideas.

II. Know the What

This is perhaps the seemingly most obvious of the 5 Ws. What you negotiate about is typically forefront in your mind as you start the dialogue. We tend to have an 'eye on the prize' approach to our negotiations in life. I'd venture to guess, though, that your sense of the *what* of your bargaining is shallower than it could be and doesn't serve you as fully as it could.

The *what* is often referred to as the 'matter' of the negotiations—the subject of your discussions, the issue(s) you're addressing (the counter to the 'means' or 'how' of the process). Most people believe they have a clear sense of this. I'm going to ask you to consider digging a little deeper.

Here are a few of the basic *what* questions that most people focus on:

➤ What do I want?
➤ What's my priority?
➤ What does the other side want?
➤ What are their priorities?
➤ What can I offer?
➤ What should I offer?
➤ What's my bottom line?

Our goal here, though, is to set you apart from 'most people'. So let's go a layer deeper. Ask yourself more *what* questions before you start bargaining.

Here's a few examples to get you thinking about the possible scope of the *what*:

➤ What leverage can I bring to bear?

➤ What strategy should I adopt?

➤ What can I say or do to be more persuasive?

➤ What unresolved personal baggage am I bringing to this discussion?

➤ What assumptions or biases do I bring that might impact on this negotiation?

➤ What other benefit(s) could potentially come from this negotiation?

➤ What impact will this negotiation have on this relationship, other relationships, future dealings, my sense of self, their sense of self, my reputation?

These may seem frivolous but can be important game-changers when applied with intention. Consider, for example, if you're negotiating with your child. You know you can easily maneuver the conversation to get what you want. But what if making your child 'up their game' while letting them 'win' the negotiation will be a great self-esteem boost and valuable life lesson for them and that the results matter very much to them but don't really matter to you. Isn't that valuable to factor in to how you conduct the negotiation? The same considerations can apply whether you're dealing with your life partner, boss, employees or otherwise—in both your personal and professional negotiations.

I remember one time, when our kids (and in particular, the boys) had been lobbying for cell phones. Our position had been that they couldn't have a cell phone until highschool at the earliest. Of course they argued that every-one else in their classes had one (which was likely true). We didn't budge despite their pleas and we clearly had the greater leverage (as they couldn't get the phones themselves). My middle guy got smart and employed some nego-tiation savvy well beyond his tender years. He crafted a letter, setting out the arguments why he ought to have a cell phone. This was no small feat. With dyslexia and other processing issues, writing was a challenge at the best of times for him. And yet he crafted a clever and compelling letter that exhibited all the hallmarks of a skilled negotiator (spelling and grammatical mistakes notwithstanding). While we had the greater leverage and could easily have maintained our position of power, it made more sense to cede the 'win' to Chase as a valuable motivational life lesson. Sometimes the 'what' that you're negotiating about is not as important as other factors that come into play.

In going deeper still in your exploration of the layers of *what*, I'd also suggest that at the outset of every negotiation, you consider what you think you're negotiating for or about… and then take a beat to explore if perhaps there is something more that underlies the negotiation. Sometimes it really is just about the 'ask' on the table. But often, there's something more behind the apparent issue being discussed. It's worth asking yourself, *is this just about the matter or thing, or is something deeper at play here (i.e., is there an issue of power, control, reputation, respect, etc.). What's motivating me or driving me on this point?*

Once you've mastered that ability, it's equally important to consider the deeper *what* vis-à-vis the other party. Think of the other party as an iceberg. What they present is only the tip. Ninety percent lurks under the surface—those all-important hidden or unstated needs.

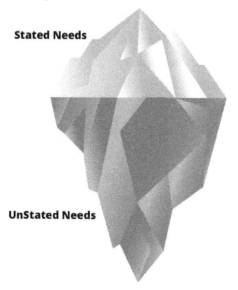

Stated Needs

UnStated Needs

Ask yourself if their 'ask' is really what it seems at face value, or are deeper issues at stake for them as well? If the answer is 'yes' (i.e., you believe other motivators are likely at play) consider whether the other side is conscious of them. Their level of self-awareness can profoundly impact your negotiations. You can tailor your strategy and tactical decisions to the fundamental motivator of your negotiating partner. It's a powerful tool. When you bring that level of insight, you can influence the negotiated outcomes by drawing on that deeper knowledge and using it to your advantage even (or especially) if the other party is unaware of their deeper drives.

Also consider what both yours and the other party's state is at the outset of your bargaining. Our state matters in negotiations, as most humans can't avoid being affected by emotions. Be intentional about what state you want to be in to maximize your influence and effectiveness while simultaneously using the other party's state to make strategic decisions about how to best approach the matter at issue.

During the negotiation, keep considering deeper-layered *what* questions, such as:

➤ What are they saying (their words) versus what they're really saying (their meaning)?
➤ What do their nonverbal cues tell me?
➤ By the same token, what messages am I sending through my tone, body language, facial expressions?
➤ What other interpretations could be read into my words?
➤ What seems to be landing well versus what's causing resistance?
➤ What tactics should I adopt?
➤ What tactics are being used against me?
➤ What other opportunities are opening up, if any?

This just scratches the surface of the multitude of *what* questions you could explore. My hope is to get you thinking about the possibilities they could open up for you. If you consider and apply the *what* of your negotiations with forethought and intention, you'll have more influence in your negotiations and get better results. It's that simple.

III. Know the Where

Now let's dive into the where—the middle child of these 5 powerful monosyllabic Ws. This is another important element of managing the environment of negotiations. Again, this factor can be considered at the macro, mid or micro level and the decisions you make will depend, in part, on the style you choose to adopt (i.e., cooperative or not) and the outcomes you seek.

My Place Or Yours?

Interestingly, people are more likely to consider the where in 'formal' business negotiations than in their personal lives. As a longtime labor lawyer, collective bargaining negotiations immediately come to mind. Parties sometimes bargain about where to bargain! It's a conscious decision about whether bargaining ought to play out on Employer's premises, Union offices or neutral territory. And so, hotels make lots of money from labor negotiations, with neither side wanting to cede perceived power.

Likewise, for corporate or legal deals, typically there's jostling for perceived advantage over whose impressive digs get showcased for bargaining. You almost expect some players to start pissing in corners to mark their territory. Sports is no exception with the real or perceived touted advantages of home turf.

Be careful not to get so caught up in the power struggle of bartering on home field that you don't consider actual strategic implications. There are pros and cons to conducting negotiations in your own space—from the business world to home insurance. Smart negotiators weigh odds to tip the balance in their favor—not based on power plays but instead grounded in practical, meaningful factors.

Being in your own space means you'll be more likely to have immediate access to information you may need, for example. This can be an advantage or disadvantage depending on the type and stage of negotiation. Sometimes there's a strategic advantage to *not* having resources available. It can allow you to defer or buy time. "I'm happy to consider that, but I'll have to check xyz and don't have access to it here." Similarly, there may be distractions to deal with in your own sandbox which wouldn't be an issue off-site.

Or consider the simple proposition that allowing someone into your space shows them a part of you that may or may not serve you. If you're trying to project an image of power and infinite resources but live or work out of a shoebox, negotiating there wouldn't be your strongest strategic move. Alternatively, if you need sympathy to drive the price down, you don't want to haggle from your multi-million-dollar penthouse suite. You get the idea.

Setting the Mood

Aside from the 'yours or mine' factor, consider the mood that would best further your cause.

- ➤ Are you trying to exert and exude power, or to make them comfortable?
- ➤ Is it a private conversation or public?
- ➤ Do you need quiet intimacy or noisy distraction?
- ➤ Is this the kind of discussion that should take place over a meal or boardroom table?
- ➤ If the former, is it a lunch or dinner issue? Casual or high end?
- ➤ Could the conversation best be tackled at a social event where the guard may be lower, or do you need the intensity of a law office?
- ➤ If the former, would a cultured event work best or something low brow?

Looking at the issue from another perspective, rooms with no windows and lacking natural light tend to drain people's energy.

These are factors you'll want to consider with intention.

Nature of the Negotiation

These considerations, in part, depend on the nature of the negotiation at hand. Where you contemplate complicated stock options or mergers and acquisitions will no doubt not be the same place you'd want to haggle your kids' curfew or even custody issues.

Even within negotiation categories, however, determining your *where*, with intention, will make you a more effective negotiator. If you're negotiating for a salary increase, for example, consider whether you'll increase your odds by raising the conversation casually at the water cooler versus the boss's office versus on a firm spa retreat. If you're bartering over the purchase of a used car, should you do it on the lot or in the office? Again, you get the idea.

Know Yourself (and the Other Party)

Considering these factors in a meaningful way also requires knowing yourself and the other party. In what setting are you most effective? Are you easily distracted and have difficulty focusing? If so, ensure your negotiations take place where you can concentrate all your attention on the issue at hand.

On the other hand, if the other party is distractible, consider whether that will work to your advantage or detract from your ability to persuade effectively. Are you most comfortable and at ease in a casual setting with a drink in your hand, or are you likely to concede more than you should in that environment? By the same token, what setting will make your counterpart most comfortable? Do you want them comfortable or will it better suit your needs if they're a little on edge?

The *where* also entails deciding whether the conversation needs to take place in person at all, or whether a phone call will suffice. And whether you determine that live or remote is most effective, always consider the possibility of recording capabilities. Today, people routinely record conversations (sometimes legally, sometimes not). Guard yourself against the possibility of surreptitious recordings in your negotiations by controlling your environment to the extent possible.

As noted earlier, people tend to be less likely to ponder the *where* as a factor in personal negotiations. So heed this advice: prepare for your personal negotiations like you would for any high stakes professional bargaining session. I caution you not to forget the *where* next time you're about to haggle with your partner or kids or other personal contact in your life. With your partner, for example, there are some conversations that can be done in the bedroom (with or without clothing), but some that need to be done at the breakfast table (especially if you're trying to sell or cast a vision for the future).

Whether in your personal or professional life or somewhere in between, these considerations can elevate the level of your effectiveness as a negotiator. Setting is important. That's why renowned authors spend so much time on setting in their books. Setting can ground or unsettle us, envelop or push us away, warm or cool us. Use it as another tool in your arsenal.

You may not always be able to control where your negotiations take place. But if you start actively contemplating the *where*, as one of the factors to consciously address in planning your negotiations where possible, you will increase your influence and get better results. Most people don't apply these factors with intention. When you do, you already set yourself apart from the pack and elevate your status as a successful negotiator.

IV. Know the When

Timing is everything. You've no doubt heard that expression a thousand times. And yet, most people still don't factor timing as an item to address with intention in their negotiations.

Tap Into Your Inner Child

As kids we knew it intuitively. Do you remember waiting until your mom or dad was in a good mood before asking for that thing you desperately wanted but knew would be an uphill battle? We instinctively tried to stack odds in our favor—line up the check marks to maximize our chances of success. When we let our eager impatience get the best of us and forged ahead despite all the warning signs, and ended up tanking our quest, we recognized our timing faux pas (although we wouldn't have called it that back then) immediately. And yet, somehow, we forget to apply this same skill as adults, when the stakes are likely higher.

When Has the Negotiation Started?

Heck, many people don't even consider when the negotiations have started. Laying the foundation in advance of the 'formal' negotiation can be a key first step to getting the results you want. Make no mistake, whether it's you or the other party setting down the groundwork, the negotiation has started at that point. If you're not aware that the other side is already negotiating, you may unwittingly be standing in the path of an unseen wrecking ball.

Prepare the Timing

Preparation is an essential element of the negotiation process. It just may be the most important element. In fact, as a basic starting point on this issue, consider it a new ground rule that the time (or when) is almost never right unless and until you're prepared.

Part of that preparation is actively considering the most strategically advantageous timing for your negotiation. Depending on the subject of your negotiation, consider time of year, month and even day or time of day. In other words, in managing the environment, consider both the micro and macro elements of timing. There's no point seeking a raise the day after budgets for the year have been finalized. Or pitching for a July family vacation the day after your only child just accepted an intensive summer internship. Asking for a bonus or perk during peak selling months is likely to be more effective than asking during winter lows. Did you just lose a big account or conversely have a record quarter? Are you a morning person or evening? What about the person you're negotiating with?

Be tactical and deliberate where possible on whether the negotiation is best served over breakfast versus dinner, or on the way out the door versus bedtime. Is this a vacation conversation, better tackled away from the distractions of everyday life? These may not seem significant, but why not maximize every possible advantage? Use the law of probabilities to your benefit.

Mood Matters

From an emotional perspective, you'll want to consider both your state and that of the other side in determining if the timing is right. For example, are you (or they) in a good mood or angry, stressed or relaxed? Are they in the middle of a big deal that's going south? If so, is that an advantage or disadvantage to getting what you want at that moment? As humans, most of us can't avoid being affected by emotions. Simply put, our state matters in negotiations. If you can control the timing, factor this in. (Or alternatively learn to control your state). Either way, be aware of the other person's state and be intentional about how that plays into the timing of your negotiation.

How Much Time Do You Allow?

Another aspect of timing in negotiations is the question of how much time you allot for the negotiations. Some negotiations shouldn't be rushed. You don't want to hurry to a conclusion to your detriment, leaving too much on the table in your haste to close the deal. By contrast, sometimes urgency is your friend in the bargaining process. Again, the trick is to be intentional. Use it with purpose.

Equally, be sure not to let the other party use time against you, by pressuring you with artificial time limits or other time constraints into negotiating against yourself or not giving yourself the time you need to fully consider your position. Have you ever rushed into an agreement that you lived to regret? Be conscious to control the *when* of your negotiations to avoid this pitfall.

Hopefully you're beginning to see the possibilities in managing the when of negotiations. This just scratches the surface of this potential minefield. The idea is just to get you thinking about these 5 Ws as serious factors to be considered and applied with forethought and intention. Sometimes, the when of negotiations is beyond our control. Life happens. Situations or opportunities arise unexpectedly. I get that. But if you start consciously considering timing as a factor to weigh, whenever possible, you'll get better results. You'll have more influence in your negotiations and increase your outcomes.

So take the time to consider time. You'll become a more effective negotiator. How simple is that?

V. Know the Why

We complete our review of these quintessential (sorry—couldn't resist the play on words) Ws as we consider the *why* of your negotiations.

Knowing yourself is one of the first steps to prepare for negotiation. A critical component of knowing yourself is knowing your *why*. Tap in to your motivation. Attaching emotion to negotiations will boost your energy, commitment and resolution. To clarify, I'm not saying to *be* emotional. I'm saying to mine and draw on the emotional underpinning that really drives a given negotiation. Let it inspire and propel you to be more persuasive and influential.

Let's consider a simple example. Imagine you're negotiating a salary increase. First, picture your approach if you believe it's just about the money. Close your eyes, and visualize how that negotiation would go down—consider your arguments, mental state, attitude, energy, and motivation. Typically, when we focus on the money our range is narrowed, both in terms of the substance we bring to the table and the process, including our emotional engagement.

Now, imagine that same negotiation, but this time, it's not just about the money. Instead, you tap into your deeper drives. Consider lifestyle benefits a salary increase brings. Perhaps it's special programming for your kids—something they desperately want but money stood in the way. Maybe a much-needed romantic (or family) vacation is what you pine for, to rekindle important relationships in your life. How about a dream adventure—a bold, bucket-list-worthy escape? If you're more of a pragmatist, is setting up a security bucket for your future and the future of your family what drives you?

And what are your whys beyond lifestyle? Maybe the salary increase signifies success, security or status for you. Does it allow you to own your value with confidence? Is it important for you to be a role model for someone and this potential salary increase is an important step in that direction for you. Maybe you want your daughter to see that a woman can succeed in a male-dominated industry, or by following her purpose and passion. The list of possible motivations is as long as the number of people negotiating every moment of every day. Consider whatever message the salary increase equates to for you.

Women often have baggage around money and wealth. This baggage can hold you back from asking for what you deserve. Money doesn't make us shallow, selfish or greedy—it helps us achieve our goals. It's important to know, with clarity, what those bigger goals and deeper whys are. Knowing your why going into a negotiation will give you greater courage, strength and impetus. It will inspire you to step in with confidence to get what you want, and to step up with the full force of your feminine power (in whatever style or means that brings to bear for you).

Once you've considered your own whys before you embark on the negotiation, it's time to turn your attention to the party you'll be negotiating with. Knowing yourself and your own motivation is only half the equation. It's critical, as an effective negotiator, to also consider the motivation of the other side. What drives them? What are their big whys? Chances are, it's not just about the money for them either. As suggested earlier, think of the other party as an iceberg. What you see and what they present is only the tip. Ninety percent lurks under the surface—those all-important hidden or unstated needs.

Using our same salary negotiation example, if you're negotiating with a manager, maybe their job security is on the line if they don't cut costs, or the bonus they need so their kid can do the once-in-a-lifetime band trip to Switzerland depends on coming in under budget. Do they need to prove to the owner that they have what it takes to take it to the next level? An owner may be driven by status, or perceived power or to prove they deserved the family business and won't let it fail. The saved money may be necessary to care for a sick loved one.

These motivations affect both the means and matter of negotiation—how they negotiate and what they're prepared to offer. Think of the advantage you hold when you know what drives them—what's really behind the posturing—what motivates their moves. You can anticipate, prepare and undercut or address these motivations. You can tailor your strategy and tactical decisions specifically to the fundamental motivator of your negotiating partner. It's a powerful tool.

And always recognize that we all want to matter. At the launch of the *Born This Way Foundation* gala, icon Oprah Winfrey had this to say on that issue:

There's a common denominator in this human experience that we all share. We all want to know that what we do, what we say and who we are, matters.[42]

This is often an overlooked *why* in negotiations and when ignored can lead to deals falling apart. At some level, we all want to be seen, validated and valued. Making the other party in a negotiation feel like they don't matter will likely preclude you from getting what you want. At a minimum, it will lead to resentment. Mastering the skill of making others feel valued in a negotiation can go a long way. I've seen people give up significant substantive rights in a deal in favor of simple acknowledgements that make them feel validated. I've also seen the other side, where people gave up reinstatement and all the backpay that goes with it rather than give an apology that made them feel disrespected.

Our *why* is attached to emotion for most people. Don't make the rookie mistake of thinking you need to stay detached. Instead, take advantage of the potential secret weapon of digging in to the emotion. Emotion is a powerful motivator. Find what motivates the other side and use it to your advantage. Find yours. Use it to fuel you. It will make you more effective, persuasive and compelling. When you understand and accept that the outcome has real meaning to you, beyond just dollars and cents, that stimulus will incentivize you and take your negotiation to the next level.

Beware though not to fall into the trap of determining your own value or worth based on the outcome of a negotiation. Getting less than you hope for in any given negotiation does not make *you* 'less than'. I've come to believe that this fear is what creates resistance to negotiation for so many (and for women in particular). It's also what drives the slippery undercurrent making navigation challenging in many negotiations and can lead to unnecessary impasse.

And so we come to the bittersweet end of our 5W journey. You've now explored how to use who, what, where, when and why as extra tools in your negotiation toolkit. My hope is to get you thinking about the possibilities the 5 Ws could open up if you consider and consistently apply them, with intention, to your future bargaining.

Think of a negotiation you've had recently
(whether personal or professional).
How could applying these 5 Ws have improved
the negotiation (either in terms of process,
outcome or relationship)?
Think of a negotiation you have coming up.
Consider each of the 5 Ws and how you can apply them,
with intention, to increase your influence, persuasive
abilities and overall experience.

If you'd like a resource to help you use my 5W model to best effect in your negotiations, grab a copy of your 5W Checklist at: www.ArtOfFeminineNegotiationBook.com.

7 DEADLY SINS OF NEGOTIATION

Now, let's tackle how to avoid the perils of the 7 deadly sins of negotiating. I'm not talking about envy, gluttony, greed, lust, pride, sloth or wrath from the Christian tradition (although avoiding those in your bargaining is also pretty solid advice). I'm talking about those simple avoidable mistakes I saw being made over and over again in my 30+ years as an attorney (and continue to see in my coaching and consulting business) that will sabotage you being able to get what you want.

I. Ego

Ego can be the kiss of death in negotiations. If you let your ego drive you, you lose control of the negotiation. You'll be easier to manipulate, less able to assess information accurately and your perspective will be skewed. You'll be less likely to recognize opportunities that may arise or alternatives that could lead to better outcomes.

Have you ever gotten into a power play with your child or loved one? When your ego kicked into gear, your negotiating skills went out the window and you dug in even though other approaches would have yielded better results? I know I have.

When you make a negotiation about you, it almost always ends poorly. Effective negotiators *listen* to determine the needs and perspectives of the other side; they don't seek to dominate the conversation. If you find yourself getting reactive and personalizing what's said (or not said) then you know your ego is in the house. When that happens, stop, breathe and regroup. Reground yourself and turn the focus back to the other party and/or the outcomes at issue.

Ego can show up in a number of ways. Let's explore a few.

(i) Need to win

If you focus on 'winning' a negotiation, you miss the point. Effective negotiation should virtually always be about securing your desired outcomes—not about beating the other party. When you focus on outdoing or getting the better of the person you're bargaining with, you lose sight of options that may be present. Your vision narrows and you lack the open mind necessary to recognize creative solutions. You become a show-horse with blinders on. Concentrating on the 'win' over your objectives ironically often leads to worse results.

Can you think of a time when your desire to win overrode your ability to find the superior solution lying on the proverbial table between you?

I remember as a young lawyer coming up against longstanding senior counsel on the other side of a high-stakes case (after having won the last few cases against him). No doubt he was embarrassed to have lost back-to-back cases against what he perceived to be an inexperienced young whippersnapper. And a woman no less! We started to negotiate an Agreed Statement of Facts. It quickly became apparent that he was determined to beat me at all costs. I took the high road, trying to come to a fair recitation of the relevant facts, but he fought on every issue, refusing to cede even the most obvious points. In fact, he'd so lost perspective that he was arguing against facts that would have assisted his position.

I finally decided to let the momentum of his approach work against him. I kept him focused on issues that were ultimately irrelevant to the real argument I intended to make. We concluded a Statement of Facts and he was smug in his belief that he'd beaten me into submission with my many purported 'acknowledgements'. And then we started to argue our cases. As I made my argument, it slowly dawned on him that our position was not at all what he'd assumed. He'd been so focused on beating me issue by issue in our negotiations that he'd omitted to include any of the facts he needed to refute my argument. The salt in the wound was that key points he needed to mount a defense were items I'd raised, and he'd rejected. I'll never forget the look on his face when he fully realized that he'd left his client completely defenseless.

(ii) Need to look good

Sometimes (but not always) tied to the need to win, is the need to look good. These buttons are easy to push, creating emotional, knee-jerk reactions that typically don't serve you as you lose perspective and weaken your position. It also leads to posturing, which is off-putting and comes across as inauthentic at best and can derail you from achieving your real objective.

Keeping your cool and keeping the big picture in mind will lead to better results. Sometimes to get to your true desired outcome, you need to look like you're giving something up along the way. If you're worried about showboating and always looking in control, you'll miss the signposts for the road to get you where you need to go.

(iii) Inability to admit you don't know

Another ego tell, often tied to the need to look good, is the inability to admit when you don't know something. Fear of looking stupid typically leads to forging ahead with incomplete information and a corresponding increased risk of bad decision-making. In addition to forcing decisions without the necessary data to make an informed choice, it can cause bluffing. Ironically, as noted earlier, most people who resist admitting they don't know something do so out of fear they'll lose credibility. In fact, the opposite is true. Bluffing undermines credibility, whereas acknowledging you don't know and undertaking to find out shows confidence.

(iv) Talking too much

Talking too much can be another sign that ego is in the room. The more you talk, the more info (and hence ammunition) you give the other party. They need only sit back, watch, listen, and pick up volumes of spoken and unspoken clues you drop on a silver platter for them.

Added to that, over-talking usually goes hand in hand with a lack of ability to listen. Active listening is a critical skill for effective bargaining and failure to listen is a huge disadvantage. Far better to listen and ask questions than control the conversation, extolling purported virtues of your position (which only reflects lack of confidence).

And let's not forget the power of silence in negotiations. If you focus on dominating the dialogue, you miss the opportunity to use silence to your advantage. Most people are uncomfortable in silence and they rush to fill the void. Using that discomfort can be a valuable tool.

(v) Wanting to be liked

Are you someone who needs to be liked? If so, beware. This is the other side of ego and will likely lead to giving concessions you ought not. People may not like the position you take, the outcome you seek, the strategy you invoke or any number of factors. You need to keep your eye on the prize, know with clarity where you want to end up, and maintain your equilibrium. Be careful not to let your desire to be liked override your need to get where you need to go.

Be on the lookout for when ego shows up in your negotiations. Be prepared to nip it in the bud.

Note that you'll want to be aware of both your own ego and the ego of the other party. In life generally, and in negotiations in particular, it can seem like we're constantly bumping up against each other's egos. Sometimes this happens intentionally. You may come up against someone who presents their ego like a battering ram, butting heads with you. If you reciprocate in kind, presenting your ego, you'll both continue to bang heads and lock horns, almost certainly losing any prospect of achieving best outcomes.

Sometimes ego-bumping happens unintentionally, more like slam dancing, where you're not intending to bash into the other party like the battering ram ego, but rather, you're both bouncing around with your egos in an agitated, high-energy state, and banging into each other as a logical consequence of that state. Or maybe it's like blindfolded Twister ego-bumping, where one or both are stumbling through the negotiation with blinders on, your egos bumping up against each other like things that go bump in the night. Raising your awareness about ego will help you avoid these eventualities and allow for better approaches and solutions.

II. Attachment

Ideally, you'll go into a negotiation with clarity around your desired outcomes. When you've prepared, you'll be able to identify your objectives with specificity. Without preparation, you risk bargaining against yourself, bargaining past your point of no return, or losing sight of your real sought-after outcome.

Presumably you're going into the negotiation because you have an objective you'd like to achieve. However, be careful not to become so attached to the outcome that you lose perspective. This is where your clarity going into the negotiation becomes key. If you can meet your desired outcome, great, but pay attention if you're not meeting your objectives. Sometimes we get so attached to the idea of getting the deal done that we continue to bargain and/or accept settlements that don't serve us. In my career I've seen countless people tank their effectiveness by being too attached to the outcome.

Have you ever had the experience where you got so attached to getting something that you ended up paying way more than you'd allowed for, and more than was reasonable? Where you'd been so attached to the outcome (i.e., getting that thing) that you lost your perspective and passed your bottom line? Or maybe it was in a relationship, where you were so attached to the *idea* of that relationship that you gave away pieces of yourself and the outcome you thought you wanted was a distant fleck in your rearview mirror. I've been there.

This model applies to both your personal and professional bargaining. I can think of countless negotiations in my law practice where I was able to get way more than our share of a deal because it was obvious the other party had become too attached to the idea of closing the deal, long past the point when it made sense for them anymore.

One case in particular stands out in my mind from early in my career. An Employer had terminated an employee, and after my cross-examination of their first witness they were nervous about their chances of success. As we engaged in settlement discussions, they got a taste of the possibility of a no-risk solution where the employee walked away permanently. Their attachment to this outcome became so obvious and so great that my client kept upping the ante to the point where the Employer paid over ten times (10X) what they would typically have been required to pay.

I've also been on the other side though. I fell in love with the property where we currently live. Growing up in a low rental apartment, I was completely captivated by the sheer sense of space that our property presented. I became too attached to the deal and continued to up our offer well past the point of fair market value. I broke the cardinal rule to never bargain against yourself. While I saw the future value of the property, and it's worked out for us, I confess that I got caught up in the moment and was not at my best bargaining self. I definitely did not practice my own No Attachment model!

Be prepared to walk away from a deal if the outcome doesn't really work for you. Trust that another deal is waiting for you around the corner. The hallmark of a great negotiator is knowing when to walk away. That certainty and confidence comes from clarity around your objectives and desired outcome at the outset. The beauty is that you don't stomp away in anger or angst, but rather, because you weren't too attached to the outcome. This is a powerful place from which to bargain.

Having said that, as per my ARE FIT model, [how to negotiate from a place of feminine power using Assertiveness, Rapport-building, Empathy, Flexibility, Intuition, and Trust], we know that being flexible is a great asset in bargaining. Not being too attached to a particular outcome doesn't necessarily mean walking away. It can also mean being open to other alternatives.

Effective negotiation isn't about winning or losing. It's not even about win/win in the sense that term is often used (i.e., a version of splitting the baby). It's about winning *better* where possible. About getting creative and cooperating to look for better results with the combined brainpower that comes from negotiating from a place of feminine power. In that mindset, be open to the possibility of exceeding your expectations. If you stay stuck in a single-minded consideration of your outcome you could miss valuable opportunities.

Being conscious and intentional about bringing 'No Attachment' to your negotiations will increase the likelihood of you securing your desired outcome... and more!

III. Reactivity

I've seen a lot of people make the fatal mistake of becoming too reactive in their negotiations. Let's talk about the importance of No Reactivity in your negotiations so you can maintain control, clarity, credibility, perspective and persuasion.

What do I mean by No Reactivity? By now you know I advocate digging for your deeper *why* in negotiations to draw on the power that comes from the emotion behind it. As noted earlier, *bringing* a deep emotional *why*, however, is not the same thing as *being* emotional in your bargaining. In fact, being emotional is often the kiss of death in negotiation.

Have you ever been really angry when you tried to bargain for something? While you were in that mode, were you able to look at things objectively? Weigh your options? Make rational, informed decisions? Keep your equilibrium? If you're like most people, the answer to all those questions will be a resounding 'no'.

Whether you're a reactive personality generally, or subject to specific triggers, I invite you to be willing to do the inner work necessary to manage sensitivities that inhibit your effectiveness as a negotiator. Being a skilled negotiator allows you to negotiate your best life. Your success as a negotiator depends, in part, on your ability to remain centered, calm, collected and compelling. If it's easy to push your buttons, you'll lose control and be easy to manipulate. By contrast, if you're able to maintain your equilibrium, you'll be more persuasive and powerful.

Some people will try to poke and provoke in bargaining. Imagine the power shift when you're able to remain unaffected by these tactics, when you remain grounded and focused even in the face of antagonism by the other party. When you don't 'blow', you deprive the other party of the wind in their sails they need to get any traction. Without your 'steam' to fuel them, they'll sputter and stall.

You may also face unintended provocations, where someone happens to inadvertently hit upon one of your triggers. Even in those cases, think of the advantage of not reacting from a place of hurt, anger, or frustration, but instead getting curious from a place of detachment and objectivity. Ask questions. Gain greater clarity. Then, you can make decisions from a place of certainty, with a view to achieving your desired outcome. Remember, walking away will be an option available to you if the other party's behavior is not worth the potential objective. But you want to make that decision from a place of clarity, not clouded reactivity.

As you can imagine, there are a few bullies in the legal profession. I found that bullying men were more apt to magnify these tendencies when dealing with a woman (with the obvious expectation that it would intimidate and throw me off my game in reactive mode). Before I tapped into the power of the Art of Feminine Negotiation, when I brought my own masculine energy to the table, I'd dish it right back and it became a contest of wills with little room for creative outside-the-box solutions.

Now, I recognize the invaluable power of not getting reactive, but instead, looking at them with genuine surprise and curiosity, seeming perplexed at their approach, and looking for the angle that will best secure my desired outcome (or better). I've left many a bully sputtering and stuttering and spewing spittle, undermining their credibility in the eyes of the adjudicator and their own client, and more importantly, undercutting their ability to evaluate and/or effectively negotiate. Taking away their power by not taking the bait is invigorating and empowering. I invite you to try it on.

As discussed under the Ego section above, if your bargaining counterpart is aggressive or inappropriate it doesn't serve you to respond in kind. Telling them to "Relax" or "Calm down" is also not a good strategy. The only time I've ever called in to a radio show contest was for the question, "What one word directive can you give to a woman that will guarantee the opposite response?" Immediately, I jumped on the phone with my answer: Relax. I won two tickets to a local show.

Instead, I invite you to ground yourself before responding. Allow your reptilian brain to adjust and release the triggered state. Take a deep breath and invoke a mantra that gives you choice in how to respond. i.e. "I'm powerfully grounded, calm, collected, and compelling." If you've done your homework and chosen your 3 words as part of your 'who you want to be' preparation from the 5W model, you can tap into your personal 3-words by substituting them for the 'calm, collected and compelling' example above. From that state, you can choose how you ought to respond.

You may choose to call out the behaviour, but not from a place of reactivity, but rather, by inviting them to be the best version of themselves. For example, you could say, "I know that treating people with dignity and respect is important to you. So, I assume you're not trying to offend or steamroll me here. Let's take a step back and reset the clock to see if we can't find a better way to reach both our best outcomes." Do you see how this allows you to take back power, while still inviting a collaborative approach?

Perception is important. It affects how others see you, react to you, and interact with you. It also affects your own sense of self. When you approach negotiations from a centered place of confidence, control, clarity, and certainty, you build rapport and trust which increases your credibility and with it your bargaining power. From that place, you are infinitely more likely to get what you want from the boardroom to the bedroom and beyond.

IV. Not Listening

A lot of people assume that the person talking the loudest and longest in negotiations is the person winning. They'd be wrong. In fact, failing to listen is definitely one of the deadly sins of negotiation.

Skilled negotiators come to their negotiations in listening mode. They know that if you're doing all the talking, you can't be learning or picking up valuable information about the other party's motivations and goals. Not only do skilled negotiators make a point of listening, but they actively elicit information through the skillful use of questions.

Let me say a word about listening.

➤ Waiting for your turn to speak is not listening.
➤ Letting someone else speak is not the same thing as listening.

➤ Thinking about and formulating what you're going to say in response is not listening.
➤ Transcribing verbatim notes is not listening.

The goal is to be an effective active listener so you can hear what people are really saying - not just their words but the full message they're communicating. This requires active listening (concentrating on the communication as opposed to passive 'hearing').

We're not taught to listen and frankly we don't have much positive modelling of this skill—especially in North American culture. The late Dr. Stephan R. Covey is oft-quoted for his observation that:

> *Most people do not listen with the intent to understand;*
> *they listen with the intent to reply.*[43]

Active listening tends to be recognized as a 'feminine' trait. Yet as more and more men and women have rejected their feminine in favor of their masculine, believing that's the way to get ahead in this 'man's' world, we seem to have lost the skill of active listening. This is to our detriment. We'd be better served tapping back in to our feminine in this regard. If you want to consider the impact of ignoring this skill in your negotiations, just think of the last time someone in your life was passive-aggressive in *not* listening to you (whether an intimate partner, child, co-worker, boss or otherwise).

For example, think of a recent example when you were trying to make an important point and the person on the receiving end was texting or scrolling through their cell phone messages, or interrupting your flow every few minutes by engaging with someone or something else going on in the room. What was your reaction? How did it make you feel (generally and toward the person in question)? Did it increase or decrease your desire to do something for the other person? How does that compare to your reaction and desire to do business with someone in your life who was attentive, engaged and positively interactive—where you felt fully heard?

Active listening takes practice. This skill is at the heart of HERsuasion.™ And it is most definitely worth the effort as it gives you the edge in negotiation.

Becoming a better listener begins with paying attention to the person who's talking to you. The trick here is to focus on nonverbal cues like tone of voice, body language, facial expressions, and momentum of speech. These nonverbal cues hint at the speaker's attitude, positioning us to empathize and meet them at their level. Picking up on whether someone is frustrated, resistant, or cheerful allows us to adapt as listeners and negotiators.

Believe it or not, noticing nonverbal cues is a lot less complicated than it sounds. You know more than you think you do! Research suggests that even babies too young to master language have a basic understanding of nonverbal communication.[44]

Beyond focusing on the speaker, be intentional with your own behaviors to show you're engaged in the conversation even if you're not speaking.

Here's some tips to improve your active listening skills:

1. Be attentive

> ➤ In other words, pay attention and give your full attention.
> ➤ Avoid distractions—both physical and mental (from avoiding environmental distractions to setting aside distracting thoughts).
> ➤ This includes 'listening' both to what they're saying (i.e., the words) and also their body language, tone, etc.
> ➤ Invoke all the senses.

2. Be *seen* to be attentive

> ➤ In other words, show that you're listening.

➤ This includes looking at the speaker and making eye contact (not staring them down but maintaining appropriate connection throughout the conversation).

➤ Use your body language to show your engagement. Ensure your posture is inviting. Lean in. Be open. Smile. Nod. Avoid crossed arms and other defensive or resistant posture and body language.

➤ Avoid fidgeting (which can be perceived as impatience, disinterest or even disrespect). Disruptions like clicking your pen or checking your phone disrupt the flow of conversation and break connection.

3. Be comfortable with silence.

➤ Always pause to allow the speaker (and yourself) to explore and collect their thoughts and feelings and to express it in their own way and time. Conversations and negotiations should not be verbal sparring matches: you don't always have to jump in, reply, or comment.

➤ Providing a moment of grace can work to your advantage.

➤ Let the other person divulge their solutions, ideas, thoughts, and concerns before you give up yours.

4. Defer judgment

➤ Stay open to truly hear what they're saying and to understand their full meaning before forming opinions or judgments about their position.

➤ Avoid 'taking sides' early in the conversation. Remain neutral and non-judgmental.

➤ Avoid jumping in with counter arguments before they've even had time to fully express their position. Interrupting is counter-productive. It limits your ability to fully understand and it frustrates and alienates the other party, thereby inhibiting creative solutions and buy-in.

5. Provide feedback

➤ Providing feedback will convey interest to the other party. This is important—remember that everyone wants to matter. Showing interest helps to achieve this end goal, which in turn will enhance the likelihood of better results.

➤ Feedback includes nodding, smiling, and saying 'mmm hmm' periodically, to encourage them to continue.

➤ Ask questions to clarify (i.e., 'What do you mean when you say …').

➤ Summarize or paraphrase what you've heard. This serves the double function of (i) showing them that you're engaged and actively listening and (ii) defusing the risk of misunderstanding. Studies show that as humans, we often misperceive the information we receive and that our perspective-taking abilities are significantly flawed. We all have personal filters, biases, and assumptions that we bring to bear without realizing. These biases can distort what we think we hear. Parroting back what you understood (i.e., 'What I'm hearing you say is …') can help alleviate this potential issue.

6. Responding

➤ Once you've listened and absorbed the speaker's ideas, look for opportunities to build onto what they've said before sharing your own perspectives and ideas. The speaker will feel respected and heard—and that will reflect positively on your patience and empathy.

Be:
➤ Calm and controlled
➤ Rational
➤ Responsive

➢ Professional
➢ Positive

Do:
➢ Keep it simple
➢ Take the high road
➢ Say what you mean and mean what you say

Avoid:
➢ Extreme statements
➢ Answering based on incomplete facts
➢ Accusing the other side of bad faith (unless necessary)
➢ Condescending or insulting the other party
➢ Personalizing arguments
➢ Interrupting the other party
➢ Abusive or profane language
➢ Becoming emotional and/or losing self-control
➢ Misleading or deceiving the other party

Active listening helps to build respect, understanding and trust while at the same time allowing you to gain valuable perspective and concrete information.

Elevated Active Listening

And now for the secret sauce. What I've come to call *Elevated Active Listening* kicks the art of active listening up a notch. When you reflect and replay back the other person's viewpoint to show them you understood it, be intentional about framing their point of view in the most generous terms possible. Make their argument even more eloquently and persuasively than they did themselves.

I recognize this may seem counter intuitive. Why would we help the other 'side' by making their argument better? I invite you to consider that that mindset comes from a conditioned perception of negotiation as a competition. Dare I say, it comes from a scarcity mindset. In fact, by contrast, when you approach negotiations from a collaborative, abundance mindset, you're more likely to get better, more creative outcomes and improved relationships.

Reflecting back someone's position in a way that is even more flattering than they articulated themselves can be a powerful way to build rapport and trust, both key elements to getting better buy-in and more creative outcomes. When I've adopted this approach in negotiations, I've seen a physical softening of the other party, a relaxing of the muscles, and a letting go of defensive postures. Invariably, it also results in triggering reciprocity wherein the other party rises to match the generosity and to better reflect back *your* position.

From this place, it is possible to come up with creative, unanticipated solutions in a way that would not arise from a place of one-upmanship or competition. Superior negotiation should conclude with an alternative that is better than had been considered by either party. In my view, this is rarely possible from an adversarial inward-focused stance but is regularly achievable when invoking elevated active listening.

Give it a try. You have nothing to lose and so much to gain.

The Art of Curiosity & Fascination

Throughout this book, I've advocated coming to negotiations from a place of curiosity. It's worth digging a little deeper into this important issue as we consider the importance of listening.

Curiosity is at the heart of being able to show up with empathy in your negotiations. It's also at the heart of rapport and trust building. It's even at the heart of releasing ego, attachment and reactivity. As you've no doubt gathered by this point, these are all foundational elements of the Art of Feminine Negotiation. So, it's worth taking a moment to put a pin in this point.

Getting intentional about getting curious will always serve you in negotiation. Make a point of asking questions. Prepare questions in advance. When you hit resistance in the negotiation, immediately switch to curiosity and turn the focus onto the other party, seeking to elicit their viewpoint, their motivations, and their underlying concerns. Continue to ask open questions, exploring, guiding, seeking to understand. In doing so, you gain valuable insights that allow you to consider creative options for resolution. At the same time, and equally valuable, you open the space for the other party to work through their own resistance.

I've had many occasions where this process has afforded *me* a new perspective that led to much more satisfying resolutions for myself and the other party. I've also seen countless cases where it softened the other party to allow them to come to see the value in my position as they were afforded the opportunity to overcome their fear of the unknown through the process. At a minimum, it allows the other party to feel fully heard, seen and respected. This is invaluable in building the relationship necessary for superior outcomes.

Tied to curiosity, I invite you to elevate the concept and approach these moments with fascination. When you release judgment and substitute it with fascination for the other party's perspective, it opens doors.

This works in professional negotiations. It also works in personal negotiations. Imagine how differently your conversation will go if you talk to your teenage child about drugs, not from a place of authority and judgment, but instead, from a mindset of curiosity and fascination. Which approach do you think is more likely to elicity honest dialogue and traction? Judgment will shut them down and create guarded reactivity, whereas fascination will open possibility for authentic sharing.

As you practice this approach, you'll develop more and more sophisticated techniques in mastering this skill. But you don't need to be a master to be effective. At the outset, it's still effective to start with simple statements like:

Tell me more about that.

I've never considered this perspective. Can you share more to help me understand?

I'm curious. Can you explain more about your concerns.

When I catch myself preaching or getting on my soapbox in a difficult conversation, I immediately pause, take a breath, and get intentional about switching to curiosity and fascination. Try it. You may be surprised by the results.

V. Jumping Straight to Business

In this busy 'to do' world, we can sometimes fall prey to the mistake of jumping straight to business. We're so focused on the end game that we fail to take time for the 'foreplay' of negotiation. As we've noted a few times, everyone wants to matter. Everyone wants to feel heard. Jumping straight to the heart of the content of a given negotiation can be jarring and uninviting. There are significant drawbacks to the 'jump in' approach to bargaining.

As we've explored earlier, 45% of the success of a negotiation can be attributed to preparation. Jumping straight to business deprives you of the opportunity to maximize this vital preparation. You want to get to know the other party before diving in to content. Easing into a bargaining session can help to do this. In fact, I'd go so far as to recommend that in many cases it makes sense to meet in advance of the negotiation and outside the formal setting. This can take the form of drinks, lunch, dinner or some other engagement that will allow you to explore the other person's motivations, interests, style, approach, thought process, and a limitless supply of other information that could prove valuable.

Think of our ARE FIT model. Jumping straight to business likely ignores most of these key bargaining skills. It doesn't allow for effective rapport-building. It doesn't build trust or give much (if any) opportunity to invoke empathy. It stifles flexibility and the creativity that comes with it. It also limits your ability to tap into your intuition as you haven't allowed yourself the chance to get a 'feel' for the other party.

The 'let's get right to it' approach also ignores the active listening principles we discussed. There is valuable insight to be mined through opening the other party to talk and through listening actively to the information garnered. Some of the most valuable advantages we gain to elevate our influence and persuasive abilities come from information we gather that is (or seems) outside the subject of the negotiation altogether.

It certainly doesn't diffuse tension or set a tone for creative cooperation, both of which are important to effective negotiating.

I invite you to explore the benefits of sliding into your negotiations instead of diving in. Start with small talk, or other personal unrelated topics to break the ice and ease any tension. Find some common ground or otherwise use methods to build rapport (see the section on Rapport-Building in the Our Secret Weapons section of this book). Be engaged. Show interest. Make them feel that they matter. Taking a few minutes to do so before 'jumping in' will make for a smoother negotiation and improve your outcomes.

VI. Lack of Integrity

Integrity is a word that gets thrown around a lot, but sadly isn't often considered with any depth. When is the last time you thought about what integrity means to you?

When we think of integrity, the first words to jump to mind are typically 'honest, moral and ethical'. Interestingly, the actual origin of the word comes from the Latin 'integritas' or integer—intact. Accordingly, often ignored definitions of integrity include: "a state of being whole and undivided"; "the condition of being unified or sound in construction"; "persons integrating various parts of their personality into a harmonious, intact whole".

What does any of this have to do with negotiating? I invite you to consider that negotiations will almost never work if integrity is lacking. This applies to both aspects of the seemingly disparate definitions noted above. Integrity is, in part, a relation you have to yourself or aspects of yourself. Integrity is also connected to how you act (i.e., whether morally). Both of these are key to how you show up for negotiating and to the results you're likely to achieve.

When we are out of integrity, we cannot show up as effective negotiators.

Let's first explore what it means to be out of integrity with yourself. This aspect of integrity is often overlooked. That is unfortunate as it's arguably the most important aspect—or at least the lynchpin to negotiating your best life. In fact, that's one of the reasons I've spent so much time in this book addressing mindset and the psychology necessary to becoming your best negotiator.

When we suffer from limiting beliefs or conditioning (as explored in the Problems section), we can't show up in integrity—i.e., in a state of being whole and undivided, unified, intact, sound or harmonious. This 'big picture' integrity issue requires you to do the necessary inner work to become whole. To recognize your inherent value. To let go of the myths and blocks that have been holding you back. To embrace your feminine strength.

Similarly, if we're not in integrity in the 'smaller picture' issues it will compromise and sabotage our ability to get what we want in our negotiations. What do I mean by 'smaller picture' integrity issues? If you're negotiating for something you don't really want or don't believe in. If you're doing what's 'expected' as opposed to what is authentic to you this will create an integrity issue and likely negatively impact on your negotiation and your outcome. If you don't believe what you're arguing, or in the fairness of your position, this too will knock you out of integrity and adversely impact on your effectiveness.

Now let's consider the second aspect of integrity—the morality of your actions. As with internal integrity, when your conduct is lacking in ethics or virtue, this will undercut your effectiveness. You will show up differently. It will create a tension that will be felt by the other party. They may not know what it is, but they will almost certainly sense the lack of authenticity. They will (if they trust their intuition) know that something is off, and it will create a discord and lack of trust that will interfere with any ability to get an advantageous deal. It often leads to tanking a negotiation altogether.

Note that with either aspect of integrity, you will not only be cheating the other party, but you will invariably be cheating yourself as well. Remember that under our ARE FIT model, 'T' is for trust. This stabilizer is key to negotiations. It's critical to build trust all ways—with yourself first and foremost and with the other parties involved. To do this requires you to be in integrity… in both senses of the word.

VII. Lack of Clarity

It may seem obvious that knowing what you want is key in any negotiation. Yet interestingly, few people dig to ensure they have the requisite clarity going into their negotiations. In failing to do so, they undercut their strength and ability to get their desired outcomes. Getting clarity is a key part of the preparation process for any negotiation. Be sure to give yourself the time to do this.

At the outset, you'll want to be clear about your motivations and your own deep 'why' (as discussed under the 5 Ws). This is an important foundation for your negotiation. And like any area in life, structural flaws in the foundation can cause the entire structure to come crashing down. I encourage you to be honest with yourself in this process. You want to get to your truth—whatever that may be. Don't let your ego, fears or 'to do' lifestyle get in the way of digging for this clarity.

Next, you'll want to get clear about your desired outcomes. When you fail to get clarity around the specifics of what you're seeking, you run the risk of the slippery slope (where you pay more or give up more than you intended and/or than is prudent in the circumstances) or of losing the deal (as you walk away from a deal that made sense because you hadn't done your homework around the range at which the deal still makes sense for you).

In addition to knowing your 'why', consider how you can apply the rest of the 5 Ws to your benefit: who, what, where and when. Get clarity on options and where you'll take a stand on each versus being flexible.

Also consider and get clarity on how you're going to apply our ARE FIT model in your negotiation. How can you build rapport? How will you bring empathy to the table? How flexible are you willing to be, and how might that look? What are some strategies you can use to build trust? For assertiveness, it's important to ensure you have clarity on the following in order to step fully into your assertiveness when necessary:

➤ Bottom Line/Reservation price/Resistance point
➤ Zone of Potential Agreement (ZOPA)
➤ Best Alternative to a Negotiated Agreement (BATNA)

[N.B. These items are each discussed more fully under Fundamentals of Negotiation]

Having clarity on these matters also helps you avoid some of the other 7 deadly sins, including issues of ego, attachment, and reactivity.

BIAS: YOUR INVISIBLE SABOTEUR

D o you consider yourself to be biased?

If you answered 'no', you'd be mistaken. We all carry biases— some conscious, most not—and bring these biases to everything we do in life. They affect most human interactions. As all of life is a negotiation, it's important to be aware of them or risk dragging your biases into every negotiation, sabotaging your chances of best outcomes.

Before you enter any negotiation, it's prudent to consider both your biases and the likely biases of the other party. To help you in that process, let's explore the types of bias, how they show up and how you can overcome them.

There are countless academic articles written on bias and various methods of categorizing bias types. The reality, however, is that many overlap and neat compartmentalizations aren't always possible. No worries though. It's not the labelling that's important. It's simply raising your awareness so you can recognize when bias is showing up and affecting how you process information. Whether you call a bias cognitive, motivational, informational, selection, heuristic, linguistic, or any of the other many assigned categories is less important than recognizing that bias is at play and getting intentional about diffusing the bias.

Let's kick-off our exploration by first tackling various personal biases and how they show up. I invite you to identify your go-to bias poisons. Explore this list with an open mind and heart with a view to recognizing your guilty bias traps.

PERSONAL BIASES

I. Self-Serving Bias

Self-serving bias shows up in a number of ways. It skews perception when we seek to perceive ourselves in an overly favorable light to maintain or enhance our self-esteem. We're all guilty of this at times. It takes a high level of self awareness and ruthless honesty to recognize when it creeps in.

It rears its head when we attribute our successes and positive outcomes to our skill yet blame our negative outcomes on bad luck (i.e., when we see our successful projects as the result of our brilliance and hard work but see our failures as the result of the team (or someone else) dropping the ball or not properly supporting the initiative). Sound familiar?

**Have you ever found yourself blaming others
when a reasonable portion of the problem
properly lies squarely at your feet?**

It also influences our perceptions of fairness. We see our positions as imminently fair and reasonable while projecting our negative attributes onto the other party. As an attorney I saw this all the time. Parties dug in to their respective positions with righteous indignation, convinced of the rightness and imminent fairness of their position. Effective negotiators need to recognize the value in the position of the other person(s) and to let the other party know they are understood as well as recognize the inherent shortcomings of their own position.

II. Egocentrism

Some see egocentrism as a subset of self-serving bias, while others see it as a stand-alone category. At its core, egocentrism shows up as tunnel vision or self-focus. This bias prevents us from truly appreciating the position of the other party as our focus is too narrowly on our own goals, outcomes, positions, etc.

This approach can cause you to tank deals that made imminent sense as you miss out on value the other party may bring to the table. This can also be the kiss of death in your personal negotiations and relationships. Unless you choose to see the needs (and value) of the other party, the relationship will suffer.

III. Inattentional Blindness

Again, some consider inattentional blindness to be the same as (or at least a subset of egocentrism and/or self-serving bias, whereas others believe the distinction warrants its own category. Inattentional bias is when we see, hear and experience only what we're focused on. When we only focus on our own needs and positions, we inevitably miss out on valuable information and insights; important cues, signals or signs; and also on opportunities.

There are variations of a powerful study that exemplifies this bias and its impact. A video is shown of a group passing a basketball, half wearing white shirts and half black. Participants are asked to count how many times the white-shirt team passes the ball to each other. Incredibly the majority of viewers fail to notice a large black gorilla jumping into the fray midway through the play. When the focus is on counting the number of passes, other glaring and obvious sensory input is missed altogether.[45]

How many gorillas have you missed in your negotiations?

IV. Overconfidence Bias

A sister to self-serving bias is overconfidence bias. This comes from a false sense of your own skill or talent. It can manifest as having an unjustified illusion of control in your negotiations. It can also show up as what's sometimes called the 'desirability effect' (i.e., what I want to happen will happen because I want it to).

There are many examples of large corporate interests that went belly-up as they suffered from a sense of their own grandiosity and turned down deals from start-ups who went on to eclipse them. Blockbuster is only one of many to meet this fate. Blockbuster was approached by Netflix but, grossly underestimating the popularity of the shift to digital viewing, turned them down only to go bankrupt shortly after.

V. Endowment Bias

Endowment bias is arguably a sister to overconfidence bias but applies to how we value what we own or what we bring to the table (i.e., when we over-value something we own or contribute).

We see examples of this in real estate deals where vendors over-value their properties (based on sweat equity or emotional attachment, etc.) and find it hard to accept market valuations. We also often see this in bartering situations where one party believes their end of the barter is considerably more valuable than what the other party brings to the table. For the same reason, many partnerships flounder as one party over-values their contribution to the relationship vis-à-vis the other party's.

Can you think of a time when you over-valued
your contribution, and it cost you?

VI. Confirmation Bias

Confirmation bias is the tendency to search for and interpret information
in a way that confirms our preconceptions. Henry Thoreau is credited with
observing that "We only see the world we look for."

The world is rife with this problem today. Social media exacerbates
this bias as news feeds we receive give us more of what we already believe.
Everyone becomes even more entrenched in their belief about the rightness of their position. This explains much of the polarization we're seeing
in politics and beyond. You are better served when you're able to show up
with an open mind to truly listen to perspectives and positions of the other
party and to seek out information contrary to your already held beliefs
(i.e., be willing to challenge your preconceptions).

VII. Expectation Bias

Tied to confirmation bias (but arguably a separate category) is what I
call expectation bias. We tend to attract what we expect. If we expect
the other party to show up as unreasonable and overly aggressive, our
perception of the encounter will meet and reinforce our expectation.
If we expect the worst, we're likely to get (or at least see) the worst,
and by contrast, if we expect the best we're more likely to get (or see)
the best.

This can show up both personally and professionally. Think of the black
sheep of the family. When everyone expects them to be a screw-up, they

invariably deliver. Beware of expecting the worst in your kids, for example. You will be more likely to see their mistakes and faux pas and in so doing create a self-fulfilling prophesy. By contrast, if you look for their gifts and encourage those, you're more likely to inspire them to step into the best version of themselves.

VIII. Affinity Bias

Affinity bias relates to the predisposition we all have to favour people who remind us of ourselves. We see this as early as elementary school yards where kids gravitate and judge more favourably those like them and tend to shun those who are different. We see this in hiring practices across the globe.

This bias causes us to discount potential valuable input, perspectives and input from those unlike us. While this is problematic in any negotiation, it is particularly problematic in cross-cultural negotiations.

Did any of these biases resonate with you?
Raising your awareness about your personal biases
is a great starting point to overcoming the adverse
impact of bias in your negotiations.

We all carry personal biases (whether conscious or not) into all our interactions. Unchecked, these biases sabotage your ability to get better outcomes in negotiating your life. They interfere with your perspective-taking ability and cloud your judgment. It's important to elevate your awareness about the inherent biases you bring to the table so you can negotiate with greater clarity and increase your influence and persuasive abilities.

Now let's turn to other types of bias that are likely showing up in your life.

OTHER BIASES

I. Information Bias

How we receive information can impact our perception and beliefs. Three primary information biases that show up are (i) Information Presentation Bias, (ii) Information Availability Bias and (iii) Misinformation bias. You can use these biases to your advantage. Beware, however, that you are not falling victim to the power of these information biases being used against you.

(i) Information Presentation

How information is presented to us can profoundly impact our receptivity to information. The advertising industry is a multi-billion-dollar industry for this reason. How we see things affects our actions (from decisions, to purchasing power, to voting and beyond). This is why large organizations or governments trying to push through a particular agenda will use fancy, glossy, high-end materials with specific language triggers etc. Be careful to ensure that your decisions are based on actual meaningful content as opposed to slick presentation tactics.

Having said that, at the other end, it will serve you to get intentional about how you're presenting information to the other party in your negotiations. A sloppily handwritten presentation with great content is likely to get less serious consideration than a professional, well-designed one with mediocre content. Also (as discussed in the 5 Ws, *Know the Who* section earlier) be sure to consider whether someone is a visual, auditory or kinesthetic learner and cater to their style(s) in presenting information that you want to ensure they consider.

(ii) Information Availability

Beware that you get access to *all* relevant information in a negotiation. It is easy to skew perceptions through strategic use of statistical or other data presented. What is omitted is often as (or more) important than what is presented. Consider and question the availability of all potentially significant information before making decisions. Pay attention to what the other party is making available and what may be conspicuously absent.

(iii) Misinformation

Tied to information availability is misinformation. Some negotiators disseminate misinformation to skew the balance in their favour. In my view, this is never appropriate. Trust is a cornerstone of effective negotiations. Breaking that trust can be irreparable. It is easier to lose trust than to build it. Ultimately our integrity needs to be our trademark. Using misinformation is out of alignment with bargaining in integrity.

Has someone ever fed you inaccurate
information in a negotiation?
How did that affect your relationship and
ability to trust that person going forward?

II. Anchoring

Anchoring is when we set expectations for a particular negotiation by starting with a strong position at the extreme edge of the range of possibility.

If we're a purchaser, for example, it serves to anchor the negotiation with a low starting price to lower the other party's expectations about what is reasonable or achievable. If we're the vendor, we'd want to anchor high out of the gate if possible.

While it seems inauthentic to proceed in this way, studies continue to affirm that anchoring can change the other party's beliefs about the nature of an appropriate agreement and so is effective in many negotiations.[46]

III. Fixed-Pie Bias

While some consider this to be a belief system rather than a bias, to some extent our beliefs *are* our biases. Our predisposed views of the world affect our perceptions and perspectives and so become biases that impact our negotiations.

Many people suffer from fixed-pie bias. They see the world and each negotiation as a fixed pie of availability where they need to ensure they get their fair slice of the pie. This scarcity mindset is to be contrasted with an abundance perspective where one believes there are potentially infinite possibilities available as solutions to any issue and seek to find the highest good for all.

Rather than fighting for the biggest piece of the pie, why not expand the pie?

IV. Framing Bias

How something is framed can significantly impact on how it is received. Being mindful of your framing can increase your ability to influence and persuade. For example, framing something as a win versus loss will invariably be better received. If someone is earning $100,000 and sought an increase to $150,000, framing a $120,000 counter-offer as an increase of $20,000 will be better received than presenting it as

$30,000 less than they'd asked for. The power of framing should not be under-estimated.

V. Sunk Cost Bias (a.k.a., Irrational Escalation of Commitment)

When we've sunk money into a particular project, person, investment, etc., studies show that we're less likely to walk away, but instead are more likely to continue to throw more money on the table as we don't want to see the money spent to date as a loss. I've been guilty of this.

When we purchased our current home it was clear it needed a lot of work. At the time, we intended to use it as a rental property and to build our 'dream home' on the lot next door. And so we renovated, but not with the high end finishes we would have invested had we thought we'd be living there longterm. We invested a lot of time and money with decent results, but it was a far cry from our personal Taj Mahal.

When we moved in (temporarily we thought), it quickly became apparent that the view from this location was unparalleled. The lot next door could never afford the level of privacy and dramatic vistas that this location provided. Now we were in a bind. The better option was to tear down the building and start from scratch, but we'd already invested a lot of resources and wasting that 'sunken cost' seemed untenable. So, we continued to throw more good money after bad, always trying to 'fix' the gaps, but never quite hitting the mark. The more we invested, the more impossible the idea of tearing down and starting fresh seemed.

The same holds true with sunk time costs. The more time we invest, the less likely we are to walk away. This can cause us to bargain long after it makes sense to do so. Many negotiators will use this knowledge as a strategy. They keep you bargaining, banking on the likelihood that the longer you stay at the table, the less likely you are to walk away. Raising your awareness about this bias and its potentially dangerous impact can be a powerful game-changer.

VI. Loss Aversion Bias (a.k.a., Prospect Theory)

For the same reasons that we don't like to acknowledge our lost investments (noted above under 'Sunk Cost Bias'), studies show that we tend to have higher aversion to losses.[47] In other words, we fear loss and avoid losses more than we try to make profits. For example, most people would rather *avoid losing* $2,000 than potentially *making* $3,000. Be aware of this bias creeping into your negotiations and causing you to make decisions that may not be the most prudent in all the circumstances.

Also, it's worth noting that as a result of this bias, how we frame offers can create a bias (either pro or con) depending on whether it's framed as a loss avoidance or gain. Use this to your advantage in your negotiations.

VII. Halo & Horn Effect

Let's face it… we tend to make snap judgments in our society. Beware though that these first impressions on meeting someone can have dangerous side-effects.

The halo effect is when a positive first impression of someone leads us to view them more favorably and cast their entire character in a more favorable light, ignoring or discounting negative attributes.

By contrast, the horn effect is when a negative first impression causes us to view them more negatively, failing to see the positive attributes.

This bias is particularly problematic in a society where we over-value attractive people and ascribe competence and other success traits to them that may not be warranted and conversely we under-value so-called unattractive people and their skills and potential contributions.

VIII. Narrative Fallacy

We naturally like stories. Humans have a long history of storytelling. As a result, we find them easier to relate to and make sense of. Pay attention though to getting sucked in to less desirable outcomes simply because they came packaged with a better story. Effective negotiators master the art of story-telling. Ask any top salesperson how powerful a well-positioned story can be. At it's core, effective advertising is a form of compelling story-telling.

At the other end, it's valuable to remember that presenting your position with a good story will get better buy-in.

IX. Hindsight Bias

Hindsight bias is the tendency to look back on events and believe we accurately predicted (or could have predicted) the outcome. This sounds innocuous, but the danger lies in our corresponding belief that our judgment is better than it is. As a result, we're less critical of our decisions going forward, which can cause poor decision-making.

X. Contrast Effect

When presented with contrasting options, most people will be inclined to choose the more attractive offer. In other words, rather than simply offering $30,000 in a deal, if presented as either $30K now or $10K/year spread over 3 years, the lump sum now will likely seem more attractive than the alternative and therefore be more appealing than the solo offer would have on its own. Presenting a contrast offer that makes your desired outcome look more attractive can create a powerful bias in your favour.

XI. False Conflict (a.k.a., Illusory Conflict)

False conflict arises where one perceives a conflict that doesn't actually exist. If we expect or anticipate a conflict or push-back, it can skew our perception so we believe we're in a conflict situation, when we're not. This will adversely impact how we show up and our ability to achieve positive outcomes.

XII. Winners' Curse

Winners' curse rears its head when we settle quickly and feel uncomfortable because it seemed to come too easily. We don't trust easy and have been conditioned to believe good things have to be hard-earned. Ironically, we end up feeling disappointed and resentful about great deals sometimes if our perception is that it came too easily.

As a result, some negotiation pundits advocate for never giving your best deal too quickly on the premise that it won't be appreciated unless the other party felt they had to work for it.

XIII. Reactive Devaluation

Similar to Winner's curse, Reactive Devaluation is when we devalue concessions given by other party simply because they were given.

XIV. Herd Mentality

Not to be confused with herd immunity, Herd Mentality is when we blindly copy what others are doing. This shows up with desires to follow famous people. It also shows up when people are drawn to follow perceived popular opinion rather than making informed individual choices. These biases can have a strong pull and can skew independent judgment and clarity of thought.

These are a sampling of the most common biases that may be holding you back from your best outcomes. Did you identify your bias poisons? If so, congratulations! You're well on your way to overcoming their adverse impact in your negotiations.

FUNDAMENTALS
OF NEGOTIATION

Now you're ready to get to some meat and bones, to explore some of the fundamentals of negotiation. It's helpful to understand the elements of negotiation to elevate your ability to get better, more intentional outcomes.

I. Means vs. Matter

Effective negotiators distinguish between the means and matter of a negotiation. It's important to consider both elements when preparing for a negotiation. Typically, we manage the means to obtain the matter.

What are means and matter?

Means:

➤ How the negotiation is conducted.
➤ Process followed.
➤ Manner in which we negotiate.

167

➤ Approaches taken.
➤ Methodology used.

This would include things like the when; where; who is included; style of negotiation; protocols; strategies; tactics; interest-based versus zero sum; etc.

Many people miss valuable opportunities by focusing almost exclusively on the matter of a negotiation without regard to the means. There can be much gained through careful attention to the means of a negotiation. Matter:

➤ What is being negotiated.
➤ Issues being negotiated.
➤ Content of negotiations.
➤ Positions taken.
➤ Terms and conditions.
➤ Substance discussed.

This refers to the 'meat and potatoes' of the negotiation, what you're seeking to achieve. Be sure to pay attention to both the means and matter when you negotiate—both personally and professionally.

II. Outcomes

Part of your preparation includes determining the outcomes you seek in any given negotiation. There are three types of outcomes to consider in any negotiation:

1. Matter/substance
2. Means/process
3. Relationship

Most people only consider or focus on the matter/substance (i.e., the 'what' of the negotiation). This is a mistake.

Sometimes it's worth sacrificing the 'what' in a particular situation to pin down the process for future dealings. Getting agreement on protocols and process can be key in long-term relationships and may benefit you far more than anything you may get in a single isolated negotiation. For example, determining how future disagreements arising from the deal will be dealt with can be a key advantage to one party or the other.

In commercial contracts, whether disputes are to be resolved in court versus arbitration can be critical. Which jurisdiction disputes are to be resolved in can give a profound advantage to a party. I've seen people sign off on deals in the United States only to find out that any disputes need to be resolved in the Netherlands. I've seen agreements which mandate arbitration in the event of a dispute and specifically identify the pool from which arbitrators can be selected. In some cases, this can severely limit one's ability to exercise their rights as the costs of a private arbitrator for a protracted hearing, in addition to potential legal costs, can be cost prohibitive for many.

In a long-term sales relationship, determining how pricing will be set may well be worth taking a loss in your first negotiated agreement if that methodology of pricing will work in your favor going forward with the bulk of the work under consideration.

Likewise, in a work situation, negotiating the methodology for compensation consideration may well justify taking less in the short run if it will lead to significant returns going forward.

It's also important to consider the outcome you seek from a relationship perspective in any given negotiation. This is probably one of the most overlooked elements of the preparation and bargaining process. How you negotiate will have some impact on your relationship with the other party.

Is this a one-off or an ongoing relationship? How you show up should, in part, depend on that. For a one-off, where you will never see the person again (like negotiating for a blanket or jewelry on the beach in Mexico) you may not worry so much about the relationship aspect of the process. However, even then, I'd caution that you may not always know in advance if your path may cross another's again. Many a time people have engaged in behavior where they thought they would have no future contact with someone only to have it come back to bite them in any number of ways. Either they did end up having to deal with the person again in the same or perhaps another capacity. Or the person knew someone who they had to deal with, so it affected their reputation and credibility. Sometimes this is known and sometimes these impacts are invisibly detrimental to us.

Also consider longer-term relationship goals or impact. In certain personal situations it may be worth giving up a little on the matter for the sake of the relationship. As discussed earlier, maybe you let your kid 'win' the negotiation with you to build their self-esteem and encourage them to self-advocate and build effective arguments on their own behalf. This can also apply professionally. Have you ever given a prospective client a smoking hot deal with a view to establishing a longer-term relationship? You get the idea.

In any event, I'd also caution that how we treat people does have consequences in a myriad of ways regardless of whether we have direct contact with them again or not.

All three outcomes are important. Be careful not to focus on one to the detriment of the others.

III. Negotiation Timeline

The actual 'formal' negotiation is only a small portion of the full negotiation timeline. Equally important are the pre-negotiation preparation time and post-negotiation debrief review time. These latter two time periods are often over-looked. That's a shame because that's where the riches lay.

Negotiation Timeline

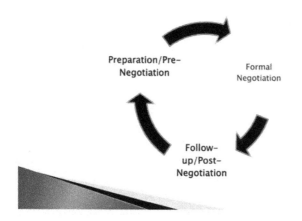

PRE-NEGOTIATION PREPARATION

P reparation is a cornerstone to any effective negotiation. In considering the elements of successful bargaining, most would say that preparation accounts for 45% of ultimate success, with leverage power accounting for an equal amount and table skills accounting for only 10%. While some quibble over the distribution of the last two elements, there's no question that preparation is a key marker for success.

Knowing how to properly prepare for negotiations will put you at a distinct advantage. It's well worth the investment. So, let's dig in to explore how to prepare for your next negotiation.

What does this preparation entail?

Know Yourself and the Other Party

This has been discussed in other sections of this book but by way of partial recap, it's important to know both yourself and the other side.

This includes consideration of strengths, weaknesses, biases, triggers, negotiation style, etc.

➤ Play to your strengths. Don't let the other party box you into a place of weakness and/or play to your biases or push your buttons.
➤ Knowing yourself and the other side also includes knowing your respective learning styles and playing to them accordingly.
➤ Know your deeper why (motivation) and that of the other party.
➤ Know what it is you want out of the negotiation—make sure to consider both short term and long-term goals and consider means, matter and relationship.

Understand Your Needs and the Other Party's Needs.

➤ Remember that both parties have needs to be satisfied.
➤ Focusing only on your own needs is typically a rookie mistake.
➤ Make a point of determining the needs of the other party.
➤ Remember the iceberg analogy—there are two types of needs: stated and hidden—the majority of needs for all parties in a typical negotiation are unstated, hidden below the surface like the mass of an iceberg.
➤ Knowing what really drives the other party can give you a huge advantage.
➤ Once you figure out the needs to the best of your ability, build your strategy around that understanding.

My No F.E.A.R. model is a valuable exercise in preparing to know both yourself and the other party in advance of your negotiations. As part of your preparation process, I advocate a quick check-in on the following 4 factors: Fear, Ego, Attachment, & Reactivity.

➤ Consider what fears are likely to show up for you and for the other party, and contemplate how you can minimize any adverse impact from these fears (or better yet, use them to fuel better outcomes).

➤ Then consider how ego is likely to show up for you and for the other party. Decide in advance how you will deal with it.

➤ Next, explore what areas or issues you may be too attached to and similarly consider where the other party may be too attached (and how you might deal with it).

➤ Finally, do a check-in about the triggers that may cause you to be reactive and, as always, consider the same for your bargaining counterpart. i.e. what triggers could cause them to become reactive and how might you take care to avoid them.

Consider the 5 Ws and How to Apply Them With Intention

Using the 5 Ws with intention will help you better navigate the negotiation process to get better results. [See How to Use the 5Ws to Up-Level Your Bargaining]

➤ As noted above, know your deeper *why* and that of the other party. Bringing that emotional motivation to the table will up-level your bargaining.

➤ Consider the *when* of a negotiation. After all, timing is everything. You can gain significant strategic advantage by choosing your timing with forethought and intention. Make time for time.

➤ Where a negotiation takes place can determine its outcome. Where possible, make this decision consciously, taking into account the pros and cons of various alternatives. Consider mood, access to information, desired comfort level, etc.

➤ Dig deeper to contemplate the many *what* questions that can impact on the relative success of your negotiations.

➤ Decide who you want to show up as. Consider your perceived role, authority, and respect. Determine who should be included or excluded from the bargaining if possible. Consider who will be impacted by the ripple effects of any deal you may strike.

Consider How You Will Bring the A.R.E F.I.T Model to the Table

As part of your preparation for any negotiation, consider, with intention, how you can best build rapport at the outset. Explore the rapport-building strategies set out earlier and decide which will best serve you in a particular negotiation.

Determine how you might bring empathy to the table. Have some questions ready so you can show up with curiosity and fascination for the other party's position.

Practice tapping in to your intuition so it is warmed up and ready to access.

Consider what strategies you can employ to build trust with the other party early in the process, to create a strong foundation from which to negotiate for best outcomes.

Get clarity on your goals and limitations so you can show up from a place of assertive graceful power.

Gather Information

➤ Make a point of determining all the possible pieces of information that could be relevant to your negotiation. Then go get it.

➤ Gather information that supports what you're seeking—whether objective (i.e., statistics, data, etc.) or subjective (i.e., anecdotal)—and also information relevant to the position of the other party.

Forewarned is forearmed. This will allow you to prepare counter-points to whatever arguments they may raise rather than getting caught off-guard.

➤ Gather information on the players in the negotiation.

➤ Gather information on those affected by the negotiation.

➤ Depending on the nature and scope of the issue(s) at hand in the negotiation, you may need to gather personal, community, industry and global information.

Set Goals and Objectives

➤ In addition to knowing your *what* for the negotiation, it's sometimes important to set interim goals (stepping stones), short term and long term objectives (both within the negotiation itself and re the consequences of the negotiation), and set priorities.

➤ Know your BATNA (best alternative to a negotiated agreement) and try to determine the other party's as well. [More on this below.]

➤ Know your reservation price and/or resistance point (bottom line for both monetary and non-monetary items alike) and try to determine the other party's. [More on this below too.]

➤ Try to determine where the ZOPA (zone of potential agreement) is likely to lie. [More on this below as well.]

➤ Plan your concessions. [Yup—more on this below too.]

➤ Determine your strategy and consider tactics that may be effective.

Analyze (issues, priorities, likelihood of success for each party)

➤ Take all the potential issues on the table and assess them. Break them down into categories where appropriate (i.e., monetary, benefits, other economic, relationship, other non-economic issues),

➤ Determine priorities as amongst each issue. Rate them high, medium or low priority.

➤ Consider your likelihood of success on each issue and argument. Rate each one optimistic, realistic, or pessimistic.

➤ Go through the same process for your expectations of the other party (i.e., assess their likely issues, categories, priorities and likelihood of success).

➤ Assess and analyze the data you've collected relevant to each party's positions.

➤ Consider your tolerances and 'pain threshold' and the tolerances of the other party.

Aspiration Levels and Managing Expectations

Under the 'Problems' section of this book, we noted that women tend to have lower aspirational levels than men—that women are less likely to think they can change their circumstances. This is important not only as a reflection of the deep adverse social conditioning that plagues women, but also for its practical impact on success in negotiations.

Studies suggest that what you want affects what you get in negotiations and that if you aim higher, you'll get more. In one study where half the control group of sellers were told to expect a settlement of $7.50 whereas the other half were told to expect $2.50, in striking numbers both groups came close to settling at the range they had been primed for.[48] In other words, those told to expect $7.50 got close to that number whereas those told to expect $2.50 only got at or around that number. Even in studies where participants got to set their own aspiration levels, those with higher expectations got more and those with lower aspirational levels got less.

While I'm not a fan of playing games in negotiations or setting artificially unrealistic end goals resulting in lengthy back and forth, it seems that reality would suggest it *is* an effective strategy. If those who set higher aspirational levels are more successful in securing higher outcomes, then it stands to reason that there is considerable value in setting high aspirations for yourself. It's important to push past your own limiting beliefs so you do not fall in the 45% of women who expect to be unable to change your circumstances.

The flip side of that coin is important to consider as well. Clearly, managing expectations of the other party is equally relevant. Coming in high (or low—depending on whether you're buying or selling for example) will set the stage to manage expectations of the other party. Lowering their expectations will increase the likelihood of you securing a better outcome.

The caveat to this is that if you go too far, you run the risk of tanking the deal altogether. The key is to find the sweet spot, where you come to the edge of your aspiration without pushing over the edge.

Know Your BATNA (Best Alternative to a Negotiated Agreement)

It's important to know your BATNA *before* going into any negotiation. And no, that's not a typo for the shoe museum. BATNA is the acronym for Best Alternative to a Negotiated Agreement. In other words, before you start to bargain, try to have a clear sense of what your options are if you don't get a deal in that particular negotiation.

What do I mean by that? Let's take the example of making a purchase (whether it's for a car, major appliance, house, or pair of shoes you've fallen in love with). If you see an identical pair of shoes at two different stores and the price is lower at one, then, assuming they both have your size in stock, your BATNA would seem to be the store with the lower price. In other words, if you know store A has the shoes for $50 cheaper and store B won't budge on price, you can walk away because you have a better option—a strong BATNA.

But what if store A didn't have your size in stock? You can still use the price at store A as a BATNA when bargaining for a better price at store B but you may or may not want to walk away if you know you can't actually get the shoes that day from store A. Or, what if store A was across town and it was an hour drive to get there, or $50 taxi ride to get there, or it was your last day in town and you didn't have time to get back to store A? Store A may *not* actually be a better BATNA, so you may not want to walk away even if you can't get the price dropped at store B. Make sense?

When you're making a purchase, you'll typically be looking at a number of factors. Price is the obvious usual suspect. So, if the item you're looking to purchase has an offered price that's above the price you know you can get elsewhere, then you have a strong potential BATNA. I say potential because there are other factors to consider in most cases (as demonstrated in the example above). People often get stuck on comparing only price and end up walking away when in fact their BATNA is not as strong as they initially thought.

Purchase of a car is an obvious example, but it's been overdone in the literature on this issue, so let's consider another option to further explore this concept. If you're bargaining for a washing machine (and yes, shopping for a car or washing machine is—or should be—a negotiation) you may find a machine for a price that looks attractive. For easy numbers (to show the concept) let's say you saw machine A for $1000. You're now looking at machine B at a competitor for $1200. On its face, it looks like machine A is a better deal. Most articles talking about BATNA advise that if you're negotiating for machine B, you know that machine A is your BATNA so if you can't get the price for B below $1000 then you would walk away because your best alternative is better. This is helpful at its basic level to demonstrate the *concept* of BATNA but it does a disservice in terms of making you a better, more effective negotiator.

Focusing only on price is too narrow a view. In fact, one of the problems in our society today is that we've all become so conditioned to look for best price above all else that production quality is dropping and it's becoming more challenging to find long-lasting quality items at all (as manufacturers/suppliers/retailers who maintain quality get squeezed out, unable to compete with what I call the 'Walmart' mentality). But that's a rant for another day.

On the issue of the BATNA for our current washing machine saga, price likely shouldn't be your only consideration. Machine A may be $200 cheaper and seem like the better deal on its face, but machine B may have a better warranty, be a better, longer-lasting supplier, or have a special delicate cycle that's missing in machine A which means you won't have to hand-wash your intimates ever again. Surely that's worth $200! And there's the point. For me, not hand-washing my delicates would be worth $200, but for you maybe not.

BATNA is often personal. What constitutes a best alternative for you will depend on how you weigh the various factors at play. There's no one right or wrong answer. Having said that, be sure to do your homework. What may seem like a great glittering BATNA at first glance may not be gold when you dig.

Insurance is a great example of this. How many times have people been lured away from their current insurance provider on the promise of better premiums (BATNA) only to find that the quote they got was subject to a whack of conditions and the premium ends up being the same or worse at the end of day. Or maybe it turns out that the key coverage you need isn't actually covered under the so-called better alternative.

Similarly, make sure your BATNA is real. If you have a job offer in hand and you're trying to decide whether to accept it, or whether to negotiate for something more, you should ensure you've done your homework in advance where possible so you're making decisions based on concrete, real alternatives—not vague hopes, dreams or expectations. Be careful not to give up a firm deal in hand for a potential BATNA in the proverbial bush.

BATNA's can provide significant bargaining power when used effectively. Knowing you have alternatives available if the negotiation falls through gives leverage. It can help determine your reservation price (your bottom line). Because BATNA's mean power in bargaining make sure you know (or at least consider and factor in) the other side's BATNA as well.

How do you determine what your BATNA is? Ideally before any negotiation, contemplate, explore, and list all the alternatives available to you if the negotiation failed. Evaluate these options—consider and weigh the value of each to you. Pick the best of those options (i.e., the one that would provide the best overall value to you). This is your best alternative to a negotiated agreement (BATNA). Now you can meaningfully set your bottom line. The more complicated the issue(s) you're bargaining, the more layered your BATNA may become, but don't panic as the principle stays the same.

Many a large, successful corporation has gone belly up because they over-estimated the strength of their BATNA and/or under-estimated the strength of the other side's BATNA. Forewarned is forearmed. Now you're forewarned. Make sure this doesn't happen to you.

Know Your WATNA (Worst Alternative to a Negotiated Agreement)

The oft-ignored sister to BATNA is WATNA. Before going into a negotiation, be sure to know your WATNA (Worst Alternative to a Negotiated Agreement) in addition to your BATNA (Best Alternative to a Negotiated Agreement). While it's important to know what best alternatives you have so you can determine your leverage going into a negotiation, it's equally important to consider your worst result if the negotiation fails.

Sometimes an unsatisfactory deal on the table may still be better than no deal at all. For example, if bankruptcy is the alternative facing you if you don't reach a deal, then getting less than your aspiration levels will still likely be better than your worst alternative to the deal. Or in collective bargaining situations, both parties must consider the relative cost of a strike if there's no deal. A deal that does not achieve some of the key items on your wish list may still be better than a strike. Make sense?

Know Your Reservation Price or Resistance Point

Once you know your BATNA (including whether or not you have one), you can then consider setting your reservation price or resistance point. Your reservation price is the minimum (or maximum depending on whether you're the 'buyer' or 'seller') amount of money that you are willing to accept in the deal. In other words, it is your proverbial 'bottom line', your line in the sand. A resistance point is the same concept, but just applied when referencing non-monetary items.

It's important to set these lines in the sand in advance so you don't get caught up in the emotion of the moment and go beyond what you intended or what's reasonable, or worse yet what you can afford. We've all had those experiences where we got swept up and gave away more than we ought to. Having a pre-determined reservation price or resistance point helps guard against these moments when our intellect seems to abandon us.

Typically, you should avoid changing your bottom line unless something has changed in the negotiation (i.e., new information arose, an unexpected power shift occurred, etc.). Having said that, always be open to exercise flexibility where warranted. This is one of the six key skill sets in our ARE FIT approach after all. Be open to better unanticipated alternatives that may present during the negotiation. But don't let yourself get pressured or rush into shifting your pre-set resistance point or reservation price without giving yourself the opportunity to consider all angles and set a new 'bottom line' in light of the information or situation.

Determine Where the Zone of Potential Agreement Lies

What is the zone of potential agreement? It's a fancy term for a simple concept. In any negotiation, there is typically a range of possible settlements. You've set your resistance point or reservation price and so has the other side (if they've done their homework). The range of overlap between what one party is prepared to pay or give and the other party is prepared to accept is the zone of potential agreement.

For example, if I was prepared to pay a maximum $5000 for a retreat facility rental and the other party was willing to accept as little as $3000 for the retreat facility rental, then our zone of potential agreement lies somewhere between $3000 and $5000. With that zone, if we're both bargaining in good faith, we should easily be able to come to a deal.

However, if my reservation price was $3300 and their reservation price was $3000, our zone of potential agreement is narrower (a $300 window) which can make it a little more challenging depending on the relative skill of the negotiators.

If my reservation price was $3000 and their reservation price was $3000, we barely have a zone of potential agreement. We can still find the deal, but it may be more challenging.

By contrast, if my reservation price was $2000 (highest I would pay) and theirs was $3000 (least they would accept) we do not have a zone of potential agreement at all and a deal is highly unlikely (unless one of us changes our bottom line).

However, in this example, where it appears we have no zone of potential agreement, if the 'seller' got creative and thought outside the box and offered me the retreat rental for three consecutive years at $2500/year and they would include morning and afternoon snacks and coffee, that might be worth me readjusting my reservation price.

Make sense?

If you want a resource to help make sure you've properly prepared for your negotiations, grab your FREE copy of our Pre-Negotiation Preparation Checklist at: www.ArtOfFeminineNegotiationBook.com

THE FORMAL NEGOTIATION

A ssuming you've done all your preparation, what are some things you may need to consider in how you handle the actual negotiation?

Opening Moves

A lot can be communicated through the opening moves of a negotiation. They can inform each side if the other party intends to be competitive or cooperative. It can demonstrate each side's view of the power balance. It can set the tone for negotiations and even tip the other side's strategy.

As noted earlier though, before you make any opening moves, be intentional about building rapport (per the ARE FIT model). Avoid jumping straight to business. Take the time to build relationship so you increase receptivity and create the space for collaborative exploration of best outcomes.

Here are a few examples of opening moves you'll typically see:

➤ Provide the other party's opening move for them
➤ Say nothing (remain silent and wait for other side to speak)

➤ Table a 'first and final offer'
➤ Set conditions before negotiating (condition precedents)
➤ Make pie-in-the-sky & multiple demands.

As noted earlier, while many (myself included) disdain the pie in the sky approach, evidence suggests that negotiators who make high demands at the outset may get better outcomes as they establish 'aspiration levels' in their favor. Having said that, I'm an advocate of getting curious right out of the gate. Ask questions to determine the other party's drivers and needs.

Early in the process, you'll want to set a high anchor for the negotiation, but then, bring your empathy to the table by getting curious and asking questions to determine the needs of the other party and gather as much information as you can to assist in finding creative options and opportunities.

How to Use Space in Negotiations

Space. Such an interesting concept. Different meanings jump to mind for different people, whether the space you live in, being spaced out, space cadets, giving each other space or proximity to others. Humans continue to be fascinated by conquering space frontiers (from the moon to mars and beyond). Heck, even monkeys have been to space. So, perhaps it's appropriate to chat about spatial consideration in negotiations (or if you want to get fancy... proxemics).

What is proxemics? The branch of study that focuses on how humans view and interpret the use of space, particularly its direct impact on behaviour, communication, and social interactions. You may have noticed that these are all elements in negotiation. So, let's consider the oft-ignored use of proxemics for improved negotiations. Mastering this concept can mean the difference between commanding a room or shrinking in it, taking control or being overwhelmed.

Let's start with those all-important personal space zones. What are they?

➤ Intimate space: the closest "bubble" of space surrounding a person. Entry into this space is acceptable only for the closest friends and intimates (however temporary or long-term they may be).

➤ Social and consultative spaces: the spaces in which people feel comfortable conducting routine social interactions with acquaintances as well as strangers.

➤ Public space: the area of space beyond which people will perceive interactions as impersonal and relatively anonymous.

Note that these personal space zones vary by culture, age, population density and even personality. We all have our own comfort zones in terms of personal space. I often joke with my daughter that she treats her intimate circle in the way others treat public space—she wants a wide berth and a protective bubble in her interactions.

Outside of personal preferences, compare a large city to a small town. In urban centres you're squished into subways, bumped on the streets, crammed into elevators, etc. By contrast, in rural communities, it's less acceptable to bump someone on the street, or sit beside them on a park bench. The size of the personal space zone increases or decreases based on the density of the population.

Another important example is the cultural differences in personal space. In many large cities in Asia, while riding the subway, it is acceptable for a stranger to fall asleep on your shoulder. In North America, this type of proximity would likely cause some discomfort.

How can you apply this in your negotiations? Consider the negotiating or bargaining space. Here are a few examples:

➤ How big is the room? Do you want to create intimacy or not? Do you want a comfortable space for the amount of people involved or not? What's the temperature? Again, are you striving for a comfortable environment or not?

➤ How does the room design impact the discussions? Are there windows, light, and airflow? This becomes an issue after hours of negotiating and can be an advantage or hindrance to effective bargaining. You may find yourself or the other party making concessions just to get out of the room.

➤ Type of chairs? This one may come as a surprise. Some negotiators try to use proxemics to their advantage by having two variations of chairs in the negotiation room, some set to a taller height than the others and/or some more comfortable than others.

➤ Table or room set up? Is the table set up in an adversarial manner, with each party on either side of the table? Although this may seem like the default seating plan, it is not necessarily the most effective for negotiations. Having members of your negotiation team sitting directly beside the other team can subconsciously increase harmonization. Also consider alternative room set-ups, whether circle or theatre style depending on the nature of the discussions.

➤ Personal space is critical: Using proxemics to understand and identify your zone during negotiations is important to guarantee fluid negotiations. Staying in the social zone is typically recommended. If you are constantly in someone's personal or intimate zone you will come off as less reasonable, more intimidating, and likely to break down negotiations. Again, however, some see this as a possible tactical move to engage.

➤ Engaging the space: Be intentional about your use of space in negotiations. Use the room to your advantage. Most people opt to stay seated, across the table from each other during formal bargaining. There can be great advantage to more fully using the space in a room, including crossing the imaginary divide between the parties.

Most people overlook this aspect of bargaining altogether. As a result, you'll be at an advantage when you bring this skill and awareness to the table (both figuratively and literally). When you're able to utilize proxemics –using space to your advantage with intention in your negotiations—you elevate your bargaining position, power, influence and results.

Strategy & Tactics

The first thing to know is the difference between tactics and strategy. People mistakenly interchange the terms.

(i) Strategy

Strategy is your overall plan for your negotiations. By that, I don't mean what you're hoping to gain or achieve, but rather, how you're going to get there. It will be determined in part by:

➤ Nature of your goals & objectives
➤ Nature of your relationship with other party
➤ Your power compared to other side

By way of example, some questions that would fall under strategy considerations include:

➤ What's my process choice for the negotiation?
➤ Are there interest-based items to discuss? Should I take a collaborative approach, looking to integrate interests for mutual gain (interest-based bargaining)?
➤ Or is this a zero-sum negotiation where we're going to 'compete' over a fixed sum/goal (distributive negotiation).
➤ Should I start with big issues or start smaller?
➤ How much more than what I want should I ask for?

(ii) Tactics

Tactics are small steps or building blocks for your larger over-arching strategy. The purpose of tactics is to alter the sense of power each party has in the negotiation. Power can be real or perceived. Used effectively, correctly chosen tactics can be a major source of power. But used poorly, they can be counter-productive.

Matter power includes things like money, authority, physical might, etc. When you don't have material power in a negotiation, you can use tactical power (means power) instead. Note that once tactics are exposed, or even identified, they tend to lose their effectiveness. So, needless to say, the idea is to recognize and identify the other party's tactics and deter them from identifying yours. Tactics can be competitive or cooperative.

You want to be careful that your negotiations don't devolve into a series of tactic/counter-tactics. Typically, authentic negotiations will always serve you better. Having said that, many people are taught or led to believe that negotiation is all about gamesmanship. The modern entertainment industry glamorizes and glorifies the use of tactics. And so, unfortunately, chances are high that you'll be faced with them at some point. You need to be aware of the range of tactics to be equipped to deal with them when confronted.

Here are some examples of sample tactics. Again, I'm not necessarily advocating any of these, but rather, I'm raising them so you'll recognize them and be forearmed. As always, remember our section on the value of integrity in negotiations. You'll notice that some of these tactics are legitimate appropriate steps whereas others are manipulative, questionable or downright inappropriate.

➤ Nibble—request more, slowly, one bite at a time
➤ Propose hypotheticals ("What if we were to …")

➤ Create fictitious issues (as trading horses for later)
➤ Bluff
➤ Delay/stall for time
➤ Leave the negotiation/walk out
➤ Set a line in the sand
➤ Set a deadline
➤ Provide an ultimatum
➤ Introduce alternative options
➤ Refer to an authoritative power
➤ Bring in a neutral 3rd party
➤ Refer to reputation and past accomplishments (theirs or yours)
➤ Request the other party's advice
➤ One-up the other party
➤ Merge several demands
➤ Divide one demand into several smaller demands
➤ Alter meeting times; frequency of meetings; duration of meetings
➤ Change venue
➤ Behave in a manner contrary to what the other side expects
➤ Split the difference
➤ Plead for special treatment
➤ Overwhelm with data/information
➤ Provide biased statistical information
➤ Play dumb—act as if unaware
➤ Revisit issues which were previously dealt with
➤ "Done deal"—act as if negotiation is a done deal
➤ Beg for mercy
➤ Appear irrational
➤ Poker face—show no emotion or reaction
➤ Emotional plea
➤ Humor
➤ Polite persistence, polite persistence and more polite persistence

How do you counter the other side's tactics?

1. Clearly identify the tactic being used against you.
2. Stop and think: what response will be most effective?
3. Carry out your response.

Possible responses to the other party's tactics:

➤ Do nothing—make a mental note of the tactic, ignore it and move forward
➤ Expose the tactic
➤ Take a break or time-out
➤ Use the same tactic back (not recommended)
➤ Ask the other party to explain why they would use such a tactic

My goal here is not to give you an exhaustive list of potential tactics, but rather, to open your perspective about the range of possible tactics available. This is valuable both so you can decide which tactics you're comfortable using and also to be able to recognize them when they're used on you.

I invite you to think about someone you regularly negotiate with (whether personal or professional).
Now that you've heard about a number of examples of tactics, think about what tactics this person has used against you in your negotiations with them.
Were you aware of it at the time or is this a new realization?
How did you react to it in the past?
Consider some options for how you'd like to handle it in future.

Using Silence in Negotiations

An old proverb says *silence is golden*. Perhaps nowhere is this more accurate than in the realm of negotiation. The exact origins of this proverb have been obscured by time and there's no consensus on when or where the saying began. One thing is sure: its pedigree is long and distinguished. Some version of the expression has been found in ancient Chinese proverbs and even Biblical Proverbs. Later variations of the expression have been linked to luminaries like Abraham Lincoln and Mark Twain, with Lincoln purportedly saying, "Better to remain silent and be thought a fool than to speak and to remove all doubt." And Twain, ever blunt, saying, "Better to keep your mouth shut and appear stupid than to open it and remove all doubt."

So why has this this expression survived history and been taken up by numerous figures and cultures throughout time? Likely because of its wisdom. I'm sure we can all think of times we wish we'd held our tongues, knowing the result would have been better had we just kept silent. Have you ever said something to a loved one that hurt their feelings and you later regretted? Even the criminal law recognizes the importance of this message, codifying a right to remain silent. So, we see that the value of silence is acknowledged in the private and public spheres, but an important (but less discussed) environment where silence is valuable, is the art of negotiations.

Silence can be a prudent course of action. It can also be a source of power. When a negotiation lapses into silence, people often get anxious and scurry to fill the silence with argumentation or tactics of persuasion. Is it good to fill the silence? Or should we remain silent? This may seem like a small question, but it can be a key factor impacting the ultimate outcome of a negotiation.

Many people wonder what silence conveys in a negotiation. Let's say you're in a two-party negotiation. If negotiations have been progressing, it's inevitable there will be a time when the other party makes their point and you're expected to respond. This is where you have a choice: fill the silence immediately or take a moment and embrace silence. It's a binary choice. You must do one or the other. We know what happens if we jump to fill the silence. We've no doubt been doing this most of our lives.

Too often, we jump in with a retort that probably would have been better if we had just thought about it for a moment. Often when we jump in, it's driven by the desire not to seem "stupid." But will people interpret your silence as stupidity, and would it really be so bad if they did?

Far from creating negative impressions, silence can be beneficial in negotiations, and if you keep quiet once the other party stops speaking, the resulting silence can be useful. For example, the silence (or pause) allows you the necessary time to absorb and appreciate what was said. This appreciation can then form the basis of a well-reasoned response, having had time to consider all, or at least more of, the ramifications that may come from accepting what the other party has proposed. In short, you can use the silence to help craft a response that bolsters your interests and best furthers your ends in the negotiation. And if the other party thinks the silence means you're stupid, well, so much the better; maybe they will drop their guard. Let your *response* dispel them of the notion you're stupid!

Stopping to think about what was said may allow you to better see things from the other party's perspective and to more fully understand their aims and interests. This can be particularly important in negotiations based on relationships, interest-based or collaborative bargaining, and ongoing or recurring negotiations (i.e., wage negotiations at your job).

Taking a moment to pause and reflect not only demonstrates that you are a thoughtful negotiator who is taking the other party's statements seriously, it shows you don't feel intimidated. When intimidated, people often scramble to speak, to assuage any conflict or perception of incompetence. Pausing to think demonstrates that you're unintimidated by conflict and won't allow your judgment to be guided by perceptions that may or may not be valid. In short, negotiators who accept silence as part of the process are less likely to be, or at least less likely to appear to be, intimidated.

More than that, your silence might even intimidate the other party! Let them be the one to squirm in the silence and perhaps rush to fill it, giving you extra information and insights to use as you see fit.

Though it seems counterintuitive, silence is a form of communication and there are times when silence can be the most effective means of communicating. Negotiation success is not based on who speaks the most, the longest or the loudest.

Of course, silence won't be appropriate all the time or in every situation. It's important to take stock if silence is the right course of action for you in any given negotiation. Don't worry about seeming incompetent. Seasoned negotiators use silence strategically. So, line yourself up in that category. Give it a shot. You might be surprised at the results.

Power of Questions

Effective Use of Questions in Negotiations

In my coaching work with my clients, I often advocate the importance of asking better questions. This starts with the questions we ask ourselves. We all tell ourselves stories, based on narratives we've carried since childhood. We continue to tell ourselves these tales even though they don't serve us. These include our stories about why we're not good enough, strong enough, smart enough, powerful enough or just plain not enough. These stories impact the questions we ask ourselves (i.e., "Why can't I ever get what I want?").

If you ask bad questions, you'll get bad answers. The good news is that the opposite is also true. If you ask better questions, you'll get better answers. I invite you to reframe your mindset so you don't come from a place of fear or uncertainty, but instead, from a place of potential and possibility. The reticular activating system of our brain is like a supercomputer. Think of it like a Google search bar. If you ask limiting questions, you'll get limiting answers. If you train yourself to ask more empowered and empowering questions, you'll get more empowered and empowering answers and so be able to lead a more powerful life.

This holds true in life… and in negotiations. Let's chat about the importance of using effective questions in negotiations. Not only can it help you get better answers, it can help build better relationships and prevent communication breakdowns. Instead of telling the other party how it should be, try finding out what they want. Sophisticated questioning will help do this.

The first step in mastering the art of effective questioning is to recognize the range of question types at your disposal.

Types of questions:

(i) Open

Ask open questions to open communication and encourage broader discussion (i.e., who, what, where, when, why, which and how). These questions do not allow for a simple yes or no response, but instead require the other side to give some real information wherever possible. The purpose is to discover the other party's needs, issues, concerns, especially those unstated hidden needs.

Some examples include:

➤ You want/need this because…?
➤ Tell me more about that…
➤ What do you need _____ for?
➤ What are you trying to accomplish/achieve?
➤ What would you like me to do and why?
➤ How would you do this?
➤ What outcome are we looking for?
➤ Would you mind explaining what you mean?

➤ What would it take to resolve this?

➤ How could we make this proposal work for you?

Ideally, when using open questions to elicit information, it's best to ensure you allow the other party to complete their thoughts before responding. In other words, don't cut them off. Don't just wait for your turn to speak. Listen carefully to the answers. There's usually gold there.

(ii) Closed

The opposite of open questions is (not surprisingly) closed questions. Utilize closed questions when you want to limit communications or control moving the discussion in a particular direction. These questions are geared to elicit a simple yes or no response from the other side. Given that the goal of negotiation is typically to try to get consensus on those issues you seek, the normal preferred use of closed questions is to try to drive the other side to give a series of 'yes' answers, leading to a yes for whatever issue you're trying to close.

Having said that, some subscribe to the theory that you want to elicit a series of 'no' answers as people are less wary about that. Whereas they're vigilant in trying to avoid agreeing with you, thinking they're giving something up, they'll be open to giving you 'no' answers. The theory is that it makes them feel in control and lower their guard.

As always, whichever strategy you use, be sure to do so with intention. Know the outcome you're looking for and design your questions to lead to that result.

(iii) Confirming

After getting an answer or information from the other party to your negotiation, it's good practice to confirm their response by asking a confirming question. At this stage, ideally you want to structure your questions precisely to get a 'yes' answer if possible. Paraphrase their thoughts from their original question.

Listen and look for key issues, themes and feelings, based on what they say or how they say it. Don't simply parrot their ideas, but instead demonstrate that you are seeking to understand. This is not the time to judge. Instead, just listen. As discussed under the 'Deadly Sin' of 'not listening', this will build rapport and trust. It allows you to seek to move their argument away from areas of disagreement by reflecting back the common ground areas of mutual agreement.

(iv) Hypothetical

Suggest possible solutions by proposing a hypothetical question. A hypothetical question allows you to consider possible options and solutions without committing yourself or pressuring the other party. And it may provide more information about the other party's needs.

When you think you have enough information about the other party's needs, then ask the other party "what if I were to do …". In this way, you can test the waters to explore potential resolutions on sticky spots while not actually committing yourself to the outcome even if accepted.

This can be an effective way to help break impasse in bargaining as it allows you to free flow ideas without the angst or pressure of worrying about committing yourself at that stage. It allows both parties to brainstorm, using the hypothetical as a launching point.

Note that some people use the hypothetical without honorable intentions. In other words, they float ideas that they have no intention of considering, simply as a means to move you off your position or otherwise mine for information for their own exclusive benefit (versus a mutually superior solution). This use is not consistent with the art of feminine negotiation in my view and accordingly, I do not advocate using hypotheticals in that way.

(v) Leading

As an attorney, this is a type of question I'm very familiar with. You've no doubt seen the objection raised in your favorite T.V. law show as opposing counsel jumps up from their seat and shouts: "Objection! Leading question!"

Leading questions are designed with the intention to lead the other person toward a specifically desired answer. They can be very obvious: "Isn't it true that ...." or "You've had problems with your current supplier, haven't you?" Sometimes they can be more subtle, just planting a tiny seed for your subconscious to grab onto. Either way, it's important to be aware of the leading question—both to use effectively where appropriate and also to be aware when someone is using a leading question on you.

(vi) Loaded

Often seen as the sister to leading questions (likely because they're also often used by attorneys and seen on leading law shows) is the loaded question. It's actually a twist on the closed question though. It's framed so as to require a simple 'yes' or 'no', but in reality, it's loaded with a purported factual underpinning that may have no foundation whatsoever (i.e., "Are you still stealing from your partner?"). Regardless of the response (whether yes or no), either triggers an implicit acknowledgment that the conduct in question did happen at some point. This is not a recommended way to build rapport or trust.

(vii) Probing

Probing questions seek to encourage a deeper exchange, designed to get the other person to further explore their answers and thoughts to take it to the next level. They are different than confirming or clarifying questions in that you're not simply seeking to ensure you understand the response, but rather, you're looking to have the other person think (or share) more deeply.

Examples include:

➤ What sort of impact do you think this will have?
➤ What are the longer-term effects?
➤ What do you see as the pros and cons of this approach?
➤ How did you come to arrive at this conclusion?
➤ What factors did you consider in choosing this option?
➤ What caused you to reject the other options available?
➤ What was your intention in proposing this option?
➤ What are you most excited about re this proposal?
➤ What's your greatest fear around this issue?
➤ What do you see as the core problem with that approach?
➤ What would you suggest we do if that turned out to be untrue?

When done skillfully, probing questions can be very effective to dig deeper so as to come up with better options and solutions. Note that tone will be key here. You want to convey genuine interest to invite the person to open up. This isn't intended to be a cross-examination or to put the other party on the defensive.

Negotiators coming from a competitive model, as opposed to practicing the art of feminine negotiation, will often err in buying into the myth that toughness carries the day and accordingly believe that keeping the other party 'on the ropes' will serve them. However, that approach does not build rapport, empathy or trust and tends to close off flexibility and inhibit any opportunity for creative solutions.

(viii) Rhetorical

Rhetorical questions are framed without expectation of an answer. They are designed to make a point. They're used to emphasize a point, to persuade, for effect, for humor, and/or to promote contemplation.

An example where a speaker used a rhetorical question for emphasis of the point is Sojourner Truth's famous "Ain't I a woman?" query.

An example where a rhetorical question is used to make a point might be "Do you think money grows on trees?"

Examples of rhetorical questions with no real answers include "Why bother?", "How many times do I have to tell you...", or "How should I know?"

The flip side of that are rhetorical questions with obvious answers, such as, "Do birds fly?", or "Do you want to live in your parents' basement forever?"

Like probing questions, they can be used to good effect or they can be used to belittle or seek to gain advantage. I invite you to use them with intention, ideally with a view to getting a better solution or result for all.

Do's and Don'ts Tips About Questions

Do:

➤ To the extent possible, plan your questions in advance of the session.
➤ Consider the impact of your question before you ask it.
➤ Ask follow up questions if necessary.
➤ Ask some questions for which you already have the answers. This helps you gauge the credibility of the other party. Consider if, when and how to inform the other party that your answer is different from theirs.
➤ Consider how you want to structure your questions (i.e., funnelling—where you start with broad questions and work to increasingly more narrow-focused questions).

Don't:

➤ Don't ask questions which are antagonistic or impugn the integrity of the other party unless you do so with intention.

➤ Don't stop listening while you're formulating your next question.

➤ Don't ask questions as if you were cross-examining in a courtroom (unless you're intending to create that mood for some benefit).

➤ Don't use questions to show how smart you are.

➤ Don't give the impression you're interested in something if you're not (unless there is a specific strategic reason to do so).

Lean In

Most people lean back from negotiations. What do I mean by that? In trying to play safe, we build in what we believe to be safeguards to minimize risk to ourselves. Yet these strategies or approaches undermine our ability to get best outcomes. Far from keeping us safe, they act as saboteurs.

We're taught to hold our cards close to our chest. We worry that if we're vulnerable, we'll be seen as weak, and others will take advantage of us. In my experience the opposite is true. That approach creates a wall between the parties – a gap or space that's tough to bridge. It doesn't lead to the transparency and trust that are necessary for creative solutions.

Humans are emotional beings. For too long, we've ignored this fact in studying best practices for negotiation. Effective negotiations are based, in part, on relationship. High EQ is a critical skill for relationship-building and hence, for effective bargaining. Yet when emotions rear up in negotiations, we usually back away, finding them messy and uncomfortable to deal with. What if, instead of backing away, you leaned in? What if you got curious? If you want to find out what the problem is so you can resolve it, you need to lean in to figure it out.

Think of an I.T. expert. When a computer acts up, spewing out info it shouldn't or freezing up or shutting down, the expert doesn't run away, but instead leans in, using that messy stuff as valuable information to make a diagnosis. I invite you to try the same in your negotiations. When those pesky emotions show up, don't back away, but lean in to the perceived problem to collect the necessary intel to identify and fix the problem.

Deal with these messy issues quickly where possible. Like a red wine spill on a white carpet, if you leave it too long the stain will be permanent, whereas if you act fast and blot, followed by a quick application of dish detergent and vinegar, you can clean up the mess and carry on with the party.

Acceptance Time

People often overlook or fail to factor acceptance time into their negotiations. As noted under 'Aspiration Levels', people come into negotiations with certain expectations. As people are generally resistant to change and as you'll be wanting to manage their expectations, you may need to allow some time for their adjustment period to the new potentially undesirable reality. We all need time to allow ourselves to adjust to unpleasant ideas or changes in circumstance. Skilled negotiators will factor this acceptance time into their negotiations.

Negotiating by Email or Other Electronic Communications

Negotiating by email or other electronic communications is an unavoidable fact of life in today's world. Whether you see the world as expanding or shrinking in the current global climate, one thing is certain. Face to face negotiations will not always be possible. In fact, technological interactions without traditional human connection seem to be on the rise. Some actually consider email to be the dominant form of communication in business today. As a result, I thought I'd be remiss not to address the issue.

There are pros and cons to this mode of negotiation, both worth noting. Let's take a look at the good, the bad and the ugly in the world of email negotiation (with some do's and don'ts thrown in for good measure). Knowledge is power and can help counter the potential negative impacts through simple strategies you can adopt to enhance the email or electronic bargaining experience.

At the outset, it's important to recognize that negotiating by email is not the same as face-to-face (or even telephone) negotiation. Ignore this simple fact at your peril. There are several pitfalls to be aware of, but first let's consider the benefits of this mode of bargaining. Email tends to give the illusion of insulation, allowing people to ask questions that may be more difficult face-to-face. Note that I've listed this under advantages although some would consider this a drawback.

A less controversial benefit is that email negotiation can clearly save time and money as it avoids unnecessary travel required with face to face meetings. It reduces stress for many people as it allows for delayed response time with the corresponding ability to contemplate and measure your reaction/response. The immediate reaction time typically required in both face-to-face and telephone negotiations can be stressful and anxiety-inducing for many and so email can be a welcome relief from that pressure. Tied to that, the additional response time can avoid the risk of explosive outbursts or ill-considered quick deals.

And yet, it's estimated that email negotiations end in impasse half the time and studies suggest less satisfaction in the process.[49] Why is that? Potential for miscommunication is an obvious culprit. While words are a fundamental means of communicating, so too are body language, facial expressions, tone of voice, and touch. All of these modes are necessary for effective communication and yet all of the latter communication modes are missing in email negotiations.

Added to that is the absence of context. In other words, there is no information other than the words on the screen. There's no ability to gauge reaction which can be a significant handicap (both in understanding the other party and in being understood yourself).

As a means of communication, email tends to elicit concise exchanges. People are less likely to engage in small talk or other personal exchanges, but rather, get straight to business. Absent potential softening that comes with in person exchanges, this style can often come across as terse, rude or confrontational. There tends to be higher likelihood of misreading tone and taking the message the wrong way. You've no doubt been at the giving or receiving end of this conundrum at some point.

In addition to the inadvertent communication mishaps, some suggest that there is a greater tendency to bluff and outright lie in email communications versus face to face encounters. The suggestion is that the screen offers a buffer that reduces accountability, empathy and concern about the bargaining counterpart's reaction (much like cyber-bullying). Arguably, with this comes less focus on mutual interests and more focus on positional bargaining. It's easier to say 'no' to a computer screen than a person.

On this theory, decreased accountability also results in agreements that don't last as parties may be more likely to back away from commitments made via email. This result may also arise as there is a tendency to prepare less for email negotiations. When not properly prepared, people are more likely to get caught with their pants down and end up making commitments that they later regret and try to resile from.

Privacy concerns also raise their ugly heads in email negotiations. Controlling access to emails can be challenging so you can never be sure who is reading the communications. Tied to that, emails constitute a permanent history of the exchange so you're never sure who is being included in the communications. With blind copies and forwarding this holds true both during the discussions and after. Not surprisingly, this can inhibit open communications.

It also makes it harder to build rapport and trust (two key elements of our ARE FIT system). Needless to say, with inhibited trust or rapport comes decreased understanding and a corresponding increase in conflict. This can be the kiss of death to effective negotiations. A corollary to that is decreased opportunity for brainstorming and creativity.

So how do we offset these risks posed by email bargaining?

It's important to make a conscious effort to find ways to establish connection. Here's 10 quick tips to help in that regard:

1. If possible, try to meet in person before starting email negotiations. This allows the opportunity to get to know each other, observe non-verbal cues, gauge reactions to each other and in so doing, build rapport.

2. In the same vein, try to build in some phone calls and/or in person meetings at some point during protracted email negotiations if at all possible.

3. Make a conscious effort to personalize the communications and add human feeling and emotion where you can. Give the other party a sense of you personally and try to elicit the same from them. Seek out common ground where you can.

4. Don't be afraid to express empathy, concern, doubt, etc. while still projecting optimism about the prospects of reaching a mutually satisfactory resolution.

5. Share personal stories or anecdotes and be sure to ask about their personal circumstances where appropriate. In other words, make small talk via email. Make the exchanges mimic 'real life' as much as possible.

6. Consider supplementing your email communications with other media.

7. At a minimum, make sure to have personalized greetings and sign-offs rather than being 'all business' right out of the gate.

8. Avoid ambiguities by making sure to ask questions early and as often as required. Also use this tactic to draw the other party into problem-solving mode.

9. Remember that email may seem rude when not intended so be intentional about not over-reacting and not responding 'in kind'. Take a

breath. Consider calling rather than emailing in response and/or to clarify. This allows you to try to keep the atmosphere positive.

10. As with any negotiation, be sure to properly prepare. Know your resistance point and BATNA going in. [Refer back to section on BATNA] Consider your strategy and what tactics you may use. Prepare for your concession strategy. [Refer back to Concession segment]

Email and other electronic communications are not going away as a means of negotiation anytime soon, notwithstanding drawbacks, so it's important to neutralize those potential pitfalls where possible and maximize your opportunity for success. Fear not. All is not lost. Words alone can obviously be a powerful means of communication as is evidenced by the many classic books that make us feel deeply and move us in profound ways. Much like those classics, however, as the authors can attest, it just takes more care and more work. But if mastering this skill can give you an edge, it's worth it, right?

It's important to similarly consider the impact of other forms of negotiation and how to best maximize preferred outcomes as technology changes our modes of communication at an ever-escalating rate. COVID has seen the dramatic rise of zoom or other video negotiations and the metaverse will no doubt soon supplant traditional meeting modes. You will want to get intentional about how to best bring some of the models we've explored to these other forums for negotiating. Ask yourself, *how can I best apply the ARE FIT and 5W models in this bargaining context? How can I ensure I build connection and trust for best outcomes?*

Concluding Negotiations : Getting to the End

We've talked about social conditioning that holds women back from stepping into their power as negotiators. We've talked, too, about the importance of preparing for negotiations and then some tactics and strategies for hands-on skills you'll need when you're in the thick of the negotiation. Because, let's face it—you can't get to the end of the negotiation and get the results you want without first going *through* the negotiation. But at some point, you have to start looking at how you move toward the end of a negotiation. Let's tackle that now.

(i) Concessions

First up on deck is the misunderstood art of concessions. Contrary to popular belief, concessions do not necessarily indicate weakness. While it's true that concession is the act of yielding, skilled negotiators strategically plan for concessions in negotiations. I'm going to encourage you to adopt this practice.

As with most things in negotiation, the key is to be intentional. Don't let yourself get caught off guard, or be reactive, or get caught up in the moment and yield things you ought not to yield. Instead, be proactive. Plan in advance. Determine what concessions you're willing to make and when. In other words, plan the *when* and *what* of concessions.

Be strategic. Negotiation is a dynamic process. Effective negotiations (especially those for long-term relationships) involve give and take. There will likely be trade-offs on both sides. Consider your priorities and the other party's likely priorities. Similarly, consider your *why* and the other side's deeper *why*. Brainstorm to come up with concessions that you can afford to give without losing your needs, or better yet, that will help you get what you really need (by meeting the other side's *why* without sacrificing your own).

Be clear in your own mind about the boundaries or limits of what concessions you can afford to offer so you don't slip past your own line in the sand. Be open to entertaining new possibilities while you're knee-deep in the negotiation but be cautious not to let emotion (whether enthusiasm or fear) outweigh your judgment. Reflect on the pros and cons and consequences before you offer up new unanticipated or unplanned concessions mid-negotiation.

Also be strategic about the timing of your concessions. Many negotiation instructors will tell you to always make the other side give the first concession. I don't agree. So long as you've done your work in advance, and planned for your concessions mindfully, you can use timing to your advantage with purpose. Depending on who you're dealing with, it may be more effective to offer the first concession and then capitalize on that.

Much like my response to those negotiators who advise to always be on higher ground than your 'opponent', it's my view that if I'm strong in my position and my preparation, then nobody is going to move me off my mark unless I want to be moved. It won't matter if they're standing above me, below me or on their head. These tactics lose their power once they're recognized and identified. So, feel free to play with the timing of your concessions—how and when you dole them out.

Having said that, be careful to manage expectations. If you offer too big a concession too early, you may signal to the other side that you don't believe your own initial demands are realistic and/or signal that there's more there. Avoid giving all your concessions too early. Pace yourself, so you have concessions in your back pocket to produce as a trade-off for something important that may come up during the negotiation. Studies suggest that people react more favorably to concessions which are doled out in increments rather than all at once.[50] It's like enjoying family holiday gifts leisurely over the course of the day rather than a mad feeding frenzy where nobody gets time to appreciate each item and moment. Pacing typically increases gratitude.

Before making a concession, consider:

➤ Is this still an issue?
➤ What's the value of this concession to each party at this stage of the negotiation?
➤ Am I giving it all when something less would do?

> ➤ Has the other party 'earned' this concession or is there immediate value for me in giving it now?
> ➤ Am I getting something in return?

Don't expect that your actions will speak for themselves and be appreciated on their own merits. Human nature often has people resist acknowledging the good deeds of others as a way to resist the reciprocity obligation. For some this is unconscious, for others intentional oblivion. Don't be shy to name your concession. Depending on the relationship, you may want to make sure you identify your concession when you offer it up—both its cost to you and the benefit to the other party.

Tied to that, always be mindful to make sure there is reciprocity. In other words, make sure the other side is giving concessions to match your offers. Don't fall into the trap of bargaining against yourself. Unless you have a good tactical reason to do so, avoid giving back-to-back concessions without anything in return. It's okay to ask for reciprocity. In fact, I encourage it if the other side isn't volunteering.

Don't make the mistake we often make as women, where we expect that our partners, kids or others will know what we want and need. Ask for what you want. Identify your concession and suggest, specifically, what you think might be an appropriate reciprocal concession. This makes sure they don't wiggle off the hook and try to take advantage, and it also increases the likelihood that you'll get what you actually want rather than wasting a concession that's of little value to you.

Know that it's okay to offer contingent concessions. In other words, if you're uncertain about the likelihood of reciprocity from your bargaining partner, then signal that you're prepared to give x if they're prepared to give or do y. While you don't want every concession to come with strings tied to pre-conditions, it can be an effective way to move forward when reciprocity is not forthcoming. Ultimately, it's about building trust and credibility.

Think about an upcoming negotiation (whether personal or professional) and brainstorm about your 'asks' and what possible concessions you could plan for (and how).

Some people see concessions as the lifeblood of negotiations. Hopefully these few tips will give you the foundation to start practicing how to use concessions to your advantage to get what you want from the boardroom to the bedroom!

(ii) Breaking Impasse

Now it's time to tackle impasse and how to break it. What is an impasse? The dictionary defines it as "a situation in which no progress is possible, especially because of disagreement."[51] Synonyms offered include deadlock, dead end, stalemate, checkmate, standoff, standstill, halt, stop, stoppage, full stop.[52] The word's origins are French, meaning unable to pass.

Clearly this is not a desired state in negotiations. The goal is not generally to hit stalemate (although there are admittedly times when this may be a strategic desired result). Even with the best of intentions, however, typically, negotiations come to an impasse at some point. So, given that the end game for most bargaining is to actually come to an agreement and get a deal, it's important to consider how to break an impasse when you come up against it.

Parties usually hit an impasse over the matter (or substance) of negotiations versus the means (or process). Although, there are certainly times when the *how* of bargaining is important enough to one or both parties that it can cause a stalemate—sometimes right out of the gate. I'm sure you've had that experience, even though you may not have thought of it as an 'impasse'. For example, if you can't agree on where or when to meet with someone, so the meeting keeps getting put off, you have hit an impasse of sorts. Most impasses, though, happens over the 'meat' of the bargaining issues.

What are some strategies or tactics to get around an impasse? Here's just a few to consider:

- ➤ Nibble approach: don't try to resolve the entire issue that led to impasse, but instead, nibble around the edges and/or take little bites towards solving the problem at hand.
- ➤ Role Reversal: have each side put themselves in the shoes of the other side—actually play devil's advocate by each arguing against your own position and for the other side.
- ➤ Record-check: put together a summary of issues agreed to date— this allows both parties to focus on the progress made rather than the stalemate and can often open up the parties to finding a creative solution.
- ➤ Future Focus: have both parties focus on the ideal future they envision if an agreement were to be reached—this refocuses energy away from the block and on the possibility and promise an agreement could bring.
- ➤ Reframe: try to reframe the outcomes as seen or perceived by one or both parties—i.e., reframe the perception from a loss to a win.
- ➤ Give and Take: ask 'what would you offer if I were to concede on this?' or alternatively consider offering something in return for their concession.
- ➤ Shift: switch the conversation away from the contentious issue that led to the impasse to allow the possibility of some forward momentum and come back to it later.
- ➤ Trial Period: propose a trial period—that way neither party is tied to a long-term buy-in, but instead can see if the proposal works or not.
- ➤ Trial Balloon: float a trial balloon by asking a hypothetical question: "What if I was to …"—that way you're not tied to the suggestion but might get some movement forward.

➤ Take a Break: take a temporary break from the negotiation and reconvene at another time.

➤ Change-up: bring in another negotiator to change the energy and momentum.

➤ No-side Neutral: bring in a 3rd party neutral to mediate.

➤ Fear Factor: have both sides share and address their respective fears—this can often be a launching point to better solutions all round.

➤ Share Stories: it's easy to say no to positions, but harder to dismiss someone's story—so, share your 'stories'/perspectives on (i) why you each think you're at an impasse and (ii) why the issue is so important to each of you—this can open up meaningful dialogue that can lead to better solutions.

➤ Set Change: change the venue—sometimes a change of scenery can change the energy and unblock one or both parties.

➤ Research and Regroup: sometimes you may need to go away and do further research and agree to regroup once you're both armed with more information and/or options.

➤ Ask, Ask, Ask: ask diagnostic questions—use open-ended questions about who, what, where, when, why and also how to dig to determine the other side's real needs, desires, fears and deeper why.

These are just a few ideas to help you get out of the box if you find yourself at an impasse in your negotiations. Ideally, you want to determine what is causing the impasse and address the root problem. Sometimes, though, good old-fashioned diversion, distraction or change-ups can do the trick.

Whenever possible, be aware of the need to allow a face-saver for the other party (and yourself if necessary). Know how to re-open talks without a loss of face for either party and without sacrificing your power. Ultimately, we all have self-interest in our bargaining. Find a way to meet the needs of that self-interest by getting creative rather than getting stuck.

Here's to busting through the barriers to get from impasse to pass through!

(iii) Deadlock or No Deal

Sometimes a deal is not to be had. Recognize this as a possibility going in. We talked about 'Attachment' as a deadly sin in negotiation. Part of being an effective negotiator includes knowing when to walk away. Don't let yourself get sucked into a deal that no longer makes sense for you.

Post-Negotiation Follow-Up

Too often I saw clients in long-term relationships (i.e., with ongoing periodic collective bargaining) finish a negotiation and shelve it, only to restart their prep as the next bargaining session commenced (sometimes years later). In the interim, they hadn't worked on or considered the next upcoming negotiation except in the vaguest possible terms. This put them at a distinct disadvantage.

As you can see from the chart at the outset of this Negotiation Timeline section, the negotiation timeline is not lateral, but rather, is a circle. It's cyclic. When you finish the formal negotiation phase, it's key to do post-negotiation follow-up. What does this involve?

Immediately following the bargaining, have a debrief session. I invite you to do so, whether it's a single bargaining session or an extended complicated series of bargaining sessions. Breakdown the elements of the negotiation and consider how each played out.

➤ What worked?
➤ What didn't?
➤ What could you do to improve?
➤ What did you learn?

➤ What areas were unresolved and therefore are still potentially alive and need to be addressed again going forward?

➤ What caught you off-guard.

➤ How could you better approach it in future?

Consider both the negotiation means and negotiation outcomes in your post-negotiation review. How was the negotiation managed from a means perspective? What did you do well? What things would you do differently? And re outcomes, measure your outcomes as against your goals. Remember to consider the 3 outcomes: matter; process; relationship.

Go back over each element of the pre-negotiation prep work and analyze it.

➤ Did you stick to the plan?

➤ Did you have to improvise? If so, why… and did it work? Why or why not?

➤ What did you miss in your prep?

➤ How can you redress that shortfall for next time?

➤ Did you apply the ARE FIT model with intention?

➤ What style(s) of negotiation did you use?

➤ Did they work? Why or why not?

➤ Did you consider and invoke the 5 Ws?

➤ What was particularly effective?

➤ What would you change to improve your results for next time?

➤ Did you fall into the trap of committing any of the 7 Deadly Sins?

➤ Did you invoke your BATNA?

➤ Did you go past your reservation price and/or resistance point? If so, why?

➤ Did the deal fall within your expected zone of potential agreement (ZOPA)? If not, where was your miscalculation or what changed?

➤ Did you make effective and intentional use of space?

➤ Could you do better next time?

➤ Did you follow your strategy?

➤ What, if any, tactics did you employ? Did they work? Why or why not?

➤ Were tactics used against you? Did you recognize them at the time? How did you handle them? Did you make effective use of questions?

➤ Where could you improve?

➤ What do you want to replicate?

In addition to the post-negotiation debrief, for any relationships where you will have ongoing engagement, from the time you finish bargaining until the next time you bargain, remember that you are still in follow-up mode. Keep track of any and all issues, concerns, ideas, etc. as they come up. Don't assume you'll remember them when the time comes. If you're like most people, you won't. Or at least not all of them. Or not accurately. Actually keep a file folder if appropriate where you can keep track of any and all pertinent information that can be of value for your next negotiation.

If you want a resource to help you debrief from your negotiations to learn from your experience (the good, the bad, and the ugly) so you can be better prepared next time, grab your FREE copy of our Post-Negotiation checklist at: www.ArtOfFeminineNegotiationBook.com

CONCLUSION

Wow! You made it. We've covered a lot of ground together. I hope you enjoyed this ride as much as I enjoyed sharing it with you. I'm excited for you as you start this new journey and experience everything that's in store for you now that you recognize the fabulous negotiator already inside you. Get set to unleash the full force of your feminine power. Now is your time.

Armed with the awareness of the problems that may have held you back—from social conditioning to blocks to fears and beyond—you can now embrace your secret weapons and take your negotiating to the next level in all aspects of your life. You can avoid the biases and deadly mistakes that plague so many negotiators and up-level your outcomes with your new handle on the fundamentals of negotiation—from pre-negotiation preparation to post-negotiation follow-up. That's something to celebrate!

I especially hope that you're proud of yourself. You should be. You made a decision to invest in yourself by picking up this book. I have absolute confidence that this investment will pay off for you 100-fold. Not only financially, but also in your relationships, your sense of confidence, the respect you'll command, the opportunities you'll be ready to go for and so much more. Enjoy your new elevated influence and persuasive abilities.

If you got value from this book, reach out—I would love to hear your story.

What's Your Next Step?

If you think you're ready to take the next step, check out our one-on-one or group coaching programs to fast-track you to the next level.

Or check out our online programs.

Consider coming to one of our incredible retreats and experience the unstoppable power of a group of women coming together to rise up.

Check out our webpage where you can book a one-on-one Breakthrough Session and to find out about our programs and also to access loads of free resources at:

www.ArtOfFeminineNegotiation.com

And make sure to join our Women On Purpose Community on FB if you're not already there:

www.facebook.com/groups/womenonpurposecommunity

You're part of our Women On Purpose family now.
Stay in touch!

ACKNOWLEDGMENTS

This book has been a passion project for me and has taken many years as its focus and shape morphed as I refined my ideas on the subject. It started with a seed of an idea about the myth that it's a man's world. It struck me that if we continue to buy into the myth that it's a man's world, we'll never truly step into the full force of our power as women. This exploration led me down a path of study on 'purpose' in life and how women so often put their dreams and passions on hold to do what's 'expected' of them.

As I dug into the ways this happens, I had a series of epiphanies. They started with the recognition that all of life is a negotiation and our first and most important negotiations are with ourselves—negotiating our mindset. And the follow-up realization that the skills that make and mark the most effective negotiators are so-called 'feminine' or 'soft' skills. So why is it that women are not considered great negotiators? Why do they buy into that myth? And so the genesis for this book was born.

As with any passion project, much thanks is due to others in my life.

I'm thankful for my father, who passed too soon, but who gave me the gift of knowing that my voice mattered and created the space to allow me to learn how to use it.

I'm grateful for my mother, who was little more than a child herself when she had my sister and I, and whose quiet strength impressed upon me the power of feminine persuasion. She intuitively knew how to negotiate an often-difficult life and modeled ingenuity and resilience as she strove to claim and exert her power.

Thanks to all the women for whom my message has resonated and who spurred me on to continue with this work.

I'm so appreciative, always, to my husband, Don, and my children, Jade, Chase and Dakota for the lessons I've learned as we grow together in negotiating our best lives.

Thanks to early beta-readers, including Wendie Donabie, Paul Feist, and Catherine Thompson, for your open, honest and heartfelt input which pushed me to always reach for more.

My gratitude also extends to our Muskoka Authors Association for the support of talented writers, passionate about the craft.

I'm so appreciative of Tyler Vibert for his painstaking attention to the endnotes (a task I don't love).

My humble thanks to Dr. Michele Williams for her gracious Foreword and to those who gave generous praise for the book, including Paul Nadeau, Isaac Betancourt, Jack Canfield, Sage Lavine and Alina Vincent.

And of course, thanks to David Hancock and his team at Morgan James Publishing for getting my manifesto out into the world.

And thanks to my photographer extraordinaire, Heather Douglas of Heather Douglas Photography for the author shots.

Thanks,

Cindy

About the Author

C indy Watson is the founder of Women On Purpose and creator of the Art of Feminine Negotiation™ and HERsuasion™ programs. She's also founder and managing partner of Watson Labour Lawyers, as an attorney specializing in social justice law for thirty years.

She is a TEDx and international speaker, award-winning author, master negotiator, and consultant known for her passion, commitment, and ability to inspire.

As a world-class women's empowerment coach, Cindy has a proven track record empowering, advocating, and motivating people to rediscover their purpose and become the best versions of themselves.

Cindy is also the award-winning author of *Out of Darkness: The Jeff Healey Story; Unloved and Endangered Animals; How to Negotiate From Fear to Powerful Resilience; and How to be a Woman On Purpose.*

Born and raised in Toronto, she currently lives in gorgeous Muskoka, Canada with her husband, three kids, and German Shepherd.

Endnotes

1   Gerzema, J. (2013, August 12). "Feminine" values can give tomor-roWs leaders an edge. Harvard business review. Retrieved from https://hbr.org/2013/08/research-male-leaders-should-think-more-like-women

2   Gerzema, J., & D'Antonio, M. (2013). The Athena doctrine: How women (and the men who think like them) will rule the future. San Francisco, CA: Jossey-Bass.

3   Diana Boesch, Elena Wirth, and Osub Ahmed, *Economic Security for Women and Families in Louisiana.* Center for American Progress. (August 8, 2019). Online: https://cdn.americanprogress.org/content/uploads/2019/08/07112848/EconSecurity-LA.pdf

4   Fact Sheet: Canadian Women's Foundation. Online: https://canadi-anwomen.org/wp-content/uploads/2018/08/Gender-Wage-Gap-Fact-Sheet_AUGUST-2018_FINAL1.pdf (updated August 2018).

5   Säve-Söderbergh, Jenny. "Gender gaps in salary negotiations: Salary requests and starting salaries in the field." Journal of Economic Behavior & Organization 161 (2019): 35–51. Online: https://econ.au.dk/fileadmin/Economics_Business/Research/Seminars/Economic_Seminars_Series/2017/Gender_gaps_in_Salary_Negotiations_NOV2016.pdf

6   "New Study Finds Gender and Racial Bias Endemic in Legal Profession." *Americanbar.org,* 6 Sep 2018, https://www.americanbar.org/news/abanews/aba-news-archives/2018/09/new-study-finds-gender-and-racial-bias-endemic-in-legal-professi/

7   Joyce Sterling and Linda Chanow, *In Their Own Words: Experienced Women Lawyers Explain Why They Are Leaving Their Law Firms and the Profession.* American Bar Association: Commission on Women in the Profession (2021). Online: https://www.americanbar.org/content/dam/aba/administrative/women/intheirownwords-f-4-19-21-final.pdf

8   Bowles, Hannah Riley, Linda Babcock, and Lei Lai. "Social incentives for gender differences in the propensity to initiate negotiations: Sometimes it does hurt to ask." Organizational Behavior and human decision Processes 103.1 (2007): 84–103. Online: https://wappp.hks.harvard.edu/files/wappp/files/social_incentives_for_gender_differences_in_the_propensity_to_initiate_negotiations-_sometimes_it_does_hurt_to_ask_0.pdf

9   Sandberg, Sheryl. *Lean In: Women, Work and the Will to Lead.* (2013)

10   Babcock, Linda, and Laschever, Sara. *Women Don't Ask: the High Cost of Avoiding Negotiation.* (2007)

11   [one example] Setty, Emily. "Meanings of bodily and sexual expression in youth sexting culture: Young women's negotiation of gendered risks and harms." *Sex Roles* 80.9 (2019): 586–606.

12   WE SHOULD ALL BE FEMINISTS by Chimamanda Ngozi Adichie. Copyright © 2012, 2014 by Chimamanda Ngozi Adichie. Reprinted by permission from Vintage Books, an imprint of the Knopf Doubleday Publishing Group, a division of Random House, Inc.

13   Sebanc, Anne M., et al. "Gendered social worlds in preschool: Dominance, peer acceptance and assertive social skills in boys' and girls' peer groups." Social Development 12.1 (2003): 91–106.

14   Leslie, Sarah-Jane. "Carving up the social world with generics." *Oxford studies in experimental philosophy* 1 (2014). Online: http://

www.princeton.edu/~sjleslie/Carving%20up%20the%20social%20world%20with%20generics.pdf

15 Danaher, Kelly, and Christian S. Crandall. "Stereotype threat in applied settings re-examined." Journal of Applied Social Psychology 38.6 (2008): 1639–1655.

16 Ambady, Nalini, et al. "Deflecting negative self-relevant stereotype activation: The effects of individuation." Journal of Experimental Social Psychology 40.3 (2004): 401–408.

17 Steele, Jennifer R., and Nalini Ambady. ""Math is Hard!" The effect of gender priming on women's attitudes." Journal of Experimental Social Psychology 42.4 (2006): 428–436.

18 Isaac, Carol, Barbara Lee, and Molly Carnes. "Interventions that affect gender bias in hiring: A systematic review." Academic medicine: journal of the Association of American Medical Colleges 84.10 (2009): 1440.

19 Fasang, Anette. "Recruitment in symphony orchestras: testing a gender neutral recruitment process." Work, Employment and Society 20.4 (2006): 801–809.

20 Forbes: https://www.forbes.com/sites/forbescoachescouncil/2020/08/03/women-ceos-highest-representation-on-the-fortune-500-list-still-isnt-enough/?sh=37f9f74b5aa8

21 Fortune: https://fortune.com/2021/06/02/female-ceos-fortune-500-2021-women-ceo-list-roz-brewer-walgreens-karen-lynch-cvs-thasunda-brown-duckett-tiaa/

22 Harvard Business Review: https://hbr.org/2021/02/women-led-startups-received-just-2-3-of-vc-funding-in-2020

23 Einarsen, Ståle. "The nature and causes of bullying at work." International journal of manpower (1999).

24 Furnham, Adrian, Emma Reeves, and Salima Budhani. "Parents think their sons are brighter than their daughters: Sex differences in parental self-estimations and estimations of their children's multiple intelligences." The Journal of genetic psychology 163.1 (2002): 24–39.

25 Porter, Natalie, and Florence Geis. "Women and Nonverbal Leadership Cues: When Seeing Is Not Believing." Gender and Nonverbal Behavior (2012): 39.

26 Kanwar, Asha, K. Balasubramanian, and Rosanne Wong. "Women Leaders in Sustainable Development." (2015).

27 Dennis, Alan R., Susan T. Kinney, and Yu-Ting Caisy Hung. "Gender differences in the effects of media richness." Small Group Research 30.4 (1999): 405–437.

28 Dijksterhuis, Ap, et al. "On making the right choice: The deliberation-without-attention effect." Science 311.5763 (2006): 1005-1007. See also: Bos, Maarten W., Ap Dijksterhuis, and Rick B. Van Baaren. "On the goal-dependency of unconscious thought." Journal of experimental social psychology 44.4 (2008): 1114-1120; and Dijksterhuis, A., (2004). "Think different: The merits of unconscious thought in preference development and decision making." Journal of Personality and Social Psychology, 87, 586–598.

29 Mayer, Roger C., James H. Davis, and F. David Schoorman. "An integrative model of organizational trust." Academy of management review 20.3 (1995): 709-734.

30 Covey, Stephen MR, and R. R. Merrill. "The One Thing That Changes Everything." THE SPEED OF TRUST. The One Thing That Changes Everything (2006): 1–40.

31 Nurjahan Boulden

32 Fenton, Richard, and Andrea Waltz. "Go for No!: Yes Is the Destination, No Is How You Get There." CourageCrafters, 2008.

33 Raelin, Joseph A. "'I Don't Have Time to Think!'(vs. The Art of Reflective Practice)." Reflections 4.1 (2002): 66–79.

34 Antanaityte, Neringa. "Mind Matters: How To Effortlessly Have More Positive Thoughts". TLEX Institute. Online: https://tlexinstitute.com/how-to-effortlessly-have-more-positive-thoughts/#:~:text=It%20was%20found%20that%20the,thoughts%20as%20the%20day%20before

35 Gazipura, Dr. Aziz, https://www.socialconfidencecenter.com/about/ .

36 Jacobson, Rae, "Why Girls Apologize Too Much". The Child Mind Institute. Online: https://childmind.org/article/why-girls-apologize-too-much/

37 Skinner, Cathleen. The effects of status and gender on interactions between parents and their children. Oklahoma State University, 2005. Online: https://shareok.org/bitstream/handle/11244/7084/Skinner_okstate_0664D_1234.pdf?sequence=1

38 Engel, Beverley, *The Power of Apology*, John, Wiley, and Sons, (2001).

39 Okimoto, Tyler G., Michael Wenzel, and Kyli Hedrick. "Refusing to apologize can have psychological benefits (and we issue no mea culpa for this research finding)." *European Journal of Social Psychology* 43.1 (2013): 22–31.

40 Ibid.

41 Wallace, Harry M., Julie Juola Exline, and Roy F. Baumeister. "Interpersonal consequences of forgiveness: Does forgiveness deter or encourage repeat offenses?." *Journal of Experimental Social Psychology* 44.2 (2008): 453–460.

42 https://www.youtube.com/watch?v=qPsuK6hsBC0

43 Covey Stephen, R., and Covey Leadership Center. *The Seven Habits of Highly Effective People: Restoring the Character Ethic*. Business Library, 1993.

44 Murphy, James M. "Nonverbal interventions with infants and their parents." *American Journal of Dance Therapy* 20.1 (1998): 37–54.

45 Simons, Daniel J. "Monkeying around with the gorillas in our midst: familiarity with an inattentional-blindness task does not improve the detection of unexpected events." *i-Perception* 1.1 (2010): 3–6.

46 Ritov, Ilana. "Anchoring in simulated competitive market negotiation." Organizational Behavior and Human Decision Processes 67.1 (1996): 16–25.

47 https://www.sciencedaily.com/releases/2020/05/200518144913.htm

48 Karrass, Chester Louis. *The negotiating game.* World Publishing Company, 1970.

49 Schweinsberg, Martin, Stefan Thau, and Madan M. Pillutla. "Negotiation Impasses: Types, Causes, and Resolutions." *Journal of Management* (2021): 01492063211021657.

50 Sanchez, Maria H., Christopher P. Agoglia, and Richard C. Hatfield. "The effect of auditors' use of a reciprocity-based strategy on auditor-client negotiations." The Accounting Review 82.1 (2007): 241–263.

51 "Definition of impasse". *Oxford University Press.* Lexico.com. 24 January 2021. https://www.lexico.com/definition/impasse

52 "Synonyms of impasse". *Oxford University Press.* Lexico.com. 24 January 2021. https://www.lexico.com/synonyms/impasse

REMINDERS ...

Thanks for joining me on this journey!

I hope you're leaving this experience ready to step into the fullness of your power.

It's also my hope that you see the potential to change the world with this approach.

Be sure to SHARE THIS EXPERIENCE with those you care about.

GIFT A COPY OF THIS BOOK to anyone you think could benefit from the game-changing shifts set out in these pages.

A reminder that this book is an interactive journey, so be sure to take advantage of the additional FREE RESOURCES to assist you in implementing the insights you've discovered in these pages, and to ensure you continue to reap the rewards going forward.

These bonuses include:

➤ Art of Feminine Negotiation Workbook
➤ FREE access to my online CONFIDENCE BOOST program

➤ Time Audit
➤ Pre-Negotiation Checklist
➤ Post-Negotiation Checklist
and more!!

Grab your extra RESOURCE MATERIALS at:
www.ArtOfFeminineNegotiationBook.com

so you can get more of what you want and deserve, from the boardroom to the bedroom.

Also a reminder to please take a moment now to leave a review of this book if you think this book would benefit other women. Your review might help another woman:

➤ Find her voice
➤ Get the recognition she deserves
➤ Make more money
➤ Improve her relationships
➤ Rediscover her life as she sets boundaries and prioritizes her dreams

A moment of your time could change a life. Share the gift of empowerment.

A free ebook edition is available with the purchase of this book.

To claim your free ebook edition:

1. Visit MorganJamesBOGO.com
2. Sign your name CLEARLY in the space
3. Complete the form and submit a photo of the entire copyright page
4. You or your friend can download the ebook to your preferred device

Morgan James BOGO™

A **FREE** ebook edition is available for you or a friend with the purchase of this print book.

CLEARLY SIGN YOUR NAME ABOVE

Instructions to claim your free ebook edition:
1. Visit MorganJamesBOGO.com
2. Sign your name CLEARLY in the space above
3. Complete the form and submit a photo of this entire page
4. You or your friend can download the ebook to your preferred device

Print & Digital Together Forever.

Snap a photo   Free ebook   Read anywhere

CPSIA information can be obtained
at www.ICGtesting.com
Printed in the USA
JSHW020838040223
37315JS00001B/9